PRA
The Enchanted Brand

"Jane Cavalier Lucas has written a must-read work for anyone in branding and business, with significant relevance beyond. She masterfully describes the need for shifting from dated traditional branding to 'enchanted branding,' which engages the human imagination like never before. Her powerful rationale and actionable steps are a game-changer."

Stephen T. Limberg, PricewaterhouseCoopers
Centennial Professor, McCombs School of Business,
The University of Texas at Austin

"Cavalier Lucas masterfully brings to light an advanced and unique brand paradigm. She cleverly illustrates new ways of thinking, innovating and adapting to an ever-changing landscape."

Debbie Rose Woloshin, chief marketing officer,
LVMH/Marc Jacobs

"Concepts such as 'serving people vs. selling to them' and 'people spending happy money' and 'empowerment based.' accompanied by meaningful elaboration, are deep-thought provokers. Jane artfully integrated her own wisdom and experience with other deep-thinkers and has created an amazing mind-stretching and important tool."

Tom Epley, chief executive of more than 10 companies
in various industries, and author of *The Plague of Good Intensions*

"Jane's unique ability to immerse herself in the culture and dynamics of an organization has no peer. Her vision, strong intellect, and unbounded energy shaped our brand and enabled us to become stewards of the whole and not just owners of the part."

Vice Admiral Joseph Dyer, USN (Ret.),
former Commander, Naval Air Systems Command

"Jane Cavalier Lucas understands brands, knows brands, and loves brands. Her special gift is knowing how they meet people because she studies and understands people's feelings and how they evolve. This book is just another powerful example. An important read for marketers who want their brands to connect today."

David Bell, Advertising Hall of Fame, chairman emeritus of the Interpublic Group, past chairman and chief executive officer of True North Communications Inc., President and CEO Bozell Worldwide

"Jane has always recognized that an organization's ability to thrive and grow is grounded in its fundamental commitment to improving the human condition. This book tells us that without imagination and innovation the most cherished brands cannot withstand the epic changes in our world today."

Sandra L. Fenwick, former CEO, Boston Children's Hospital

"How can companies and their brands navigate our world of incessant, frenzied, tectonic shifts? *The Enchanted Brand* answers with a wild ride of inspirational insights and clever strategy, drawn from areas as diverse as military tactics, psychology, consumerism, and, of course, marketing. A transcendent read full of practical advice and perspective."

Preston McAfee, Google Distinguished Scientist

"I entreat every CEO to read this book because what you don't know, especially in today's world, can really hurt you. If you want to find out what mind nourishment, sad money, culture jamming, the scary new, fan fiction, and open stories are read this book. This book is not for the faint of heart, but companies and CEO's that want to be at the heart of a new and necessary tomorrow."

Joey Cummings, recognized as Fortune Magazine People to Watch and Advertising Age 100 Best Creatives

"Reading this book forever changed my view of brand and its unleashed purpose and power in today and tomorrow's world. Truly inspiring and thought provoking."

Robert Riney, president, Healthcare Operations and chief operating officer, Henry Ford Health System

"I have had the pleasure of working with Jane Cavalier Lucas to successfully brand and rebrand a number of highly successful ventures. Having seen her in the trenches of building brands, I can say that this book captures and commits to writing her methodology of finding and communicating the spirit of a brand in a way that empowers the branding practitioner to execute the magic without possessing Jane's sixth sense for doing so. It is one thing to know how to brand, it is another thing entirely to be able to explain how. That is exactly what Jane has done here."

Sam Havelock, founder and CEO of SOFX Inc., chief brand officer, Gatorz Eyewear, Navy Seal Commander (Ret.)

"Whether you are a CEO or a gig worker, *The Enchanted Brand* masterfully provides a practical blueprint for creating a brand that authentically connects with your people. As a foremost expert on the power of branding, Jane beautifully explains how, in a changing and uncertain world, enchanted brands can bring joy, inspiration and solace to your customers—creating a stronger, more loyal and lasting relationship."

Corinne Basler, chairwoman Perkins School for the Blind, board member Save the Children

"This book does a great job of getting you see the world in a new way and understand how brands can meet the new needs of people living under unrelenting disruptive change."

Terri Kelly, retired president and CEO of W. L. Gore & Associates

"*The Enchanted Brand* is an essential guide for any brand that's ready to confront how much and how quickly the world is changing and focus not on selling more stuff, but on serving people and giving them the tools to embrace their humanity and achieve happiness."

Peter Rojas, founder of Gizmodo and Engadget
and Partner BetaVentures

"Having personally benefited from Jane Cavalier Lucas's unique talent and insight as a corporate and academic leader within two organizations, I'm not at all surprised that she has hit the bullseye once again. *The Enchanted Brand* shows Jane is, as always, ahead of the curve, redefining the meaning and power of "brand" to declare the distinctive value of your company or organization — both within and without. Enchanted Brands is both brilliant and truly useful."

Dr. Susan Marquis, Charles and Marie Robertson Visiting Professor Princeton University, RAND VP of Innovation and Dean Pardee RAND Graduate School (former), author *I Am Not a Tractor* (Cornell University Press), *Unconventional Warfare: Rebuilding U.S. Operations Forces* (Brookings Institution Press)

"Most books about brands offer little insight because they are written as rear view mirror observations. With 20/20 hindsight, they opine about which brands have been historically successful and why.

In contrast, in Jane Cavalier Lucas's book *The Enchanted Brand*, she has aggregated her vast experience, knowledge and insight to offer a fascinating vision of how brands will be important and should be thought of in the future. It is a thought-provoking and relevant read for all businesses."

Bruce Kelley, retired vice chairman, the Martin Agency

THE ENCHANTED BRAND

Strengthening the Human Side of Business in the Age of New Essentialism

JANE CAVALIER LUCAS

INDIE BOOKS
INTERNATIONAL

ISBN-13: 978-1-952233-79-1
Library of Congress Control Number: 2021921585
Interior designed by Bill Ramsey
Book cover created by Amber Gans-Periera
Additional illustrations and graphics are by Amber Gans-Periera

INDIE BOOKS INTERNATIONAL, INC.®
2424 VISTA WAY, SUITE 316
OCEANSIDE, CA 92054
www.indiebooksintl.com

Dedication

*This work is dedicated to my husband Scott
and our three children Justin, Halle, and Daniel,
who have enchanted me since they were born.*

Table of Contents

Introduction iii

Part I: A World in Metamorphosis

1. From Caterpillar to Butterfly 1
2. Unbridled Consumerism to New Essentialism. 15
3. The Search for New Coherence: The Struggle to
Understand the Unthinkable Effects of Metamorphosis. . . .39
4. The Human Side of Business:
People Must Come First 49
5. Enchantment Is the Answer:
Thriving in a VUCA World. 55

Part II: Creating an Enchanted Brand

6. Brand Basics: What Is a Brand
and How Does It Work?. 65
7. Brand Basics—Your Brand Can Be A Priceless Asset 79
8. Building an Enchanted Brand 93
9. The Enchanted Brand Gallery 125
10. Rebranding To Become Enchanted 135
11. How to Create an Enchanted Brand Culture. 159
12. Enchanting Your Personal Professional Brand 175
13. Branding in a Networked World 187

Part III: Bringing Enchantment into Your Life and the World

14. Seven Steps to Bring More Enchantment
into Your Life 205
15. Building a Better World with Enchanted Brands 209

Bibliography 221
Acknowledgments. 233
About The Author 235
Trademark Brands Referenced. 237
Endnotes 247
Index 259

Introduction

IN 1993 IN MOGADISHU, WHILE ON A JOINT UNITED STATES Special Operations mission to capture warlord Mohammed Farah Aidid and other militants responsible for attacks on American and U.N. personnel in Somalia, two Black Hawk helicopters were shot down by Somali forces. A battle to defend the survivors of the downed helicopters raged throughout the night, and when it was over, eighteen American Special Operations servicemen had died, eighty were wounded and hundreds of Somalis perished. A decade after the battle of Mogadishu, when General Stanley McChrystal became the commander of Joint Special Operations Command (JSOC), he looked back at this event as the moment that the old bureaucratic structure failed within the new, networked world.

McChrystal realized that it takes a network to defeat a network, and he set about re-imaging and redesigning virtually everything under his command along a network framework. He focused on discovering what would amplify the agency of his troops in a modern, technology-enhanced world. He embraced interdependence, emergence (when things come together and something unexpected is created), speed and rhythm (controlling the pace and timing to create a difference outcome), blending action and intelligence (bringing in the intelligence community to collect information as part of a mission), creating a shared consciousness, and staying fluid when reacting to emerging events. During his command at the JSOC in the mid-2000s, McChrystal went from ten to fourteen missions a month to 300 successful operations a month, with greater precision and intelligence yield, by casting aside a century of conventional wisdom and adapting to a radically new world.[1]

The above story illustrates the need for drastic shifts in approach when confronted with drastic changes in an operating environment. In the operating environment of our new world, I propose that individuals, organizations, and humanity better thrive by strengthening use of the imagination, and that Enchanted Brands are imagination-stimulators that empower human performance. By populating organizational and social cultures with Enchanted Brands, we empower people to go beyond the complexity, uncertainty, ambiguity and constant changes of life, to adapt and grow.

The human experience is changing right in front of us. Consider how people are increasingly marginalized by technologies that dehumanize and distort reality. From constant algorithmic communications to digital tracking and privacy invasions to using our profiles to echo our own ideas (creating the illusion-delusion that the whole world shares our ideas) to making decisions for us automatically and telling us what to hear (yes, Alexa that's you), we are being subjugated, manipulated, and played.

What happens when our complex society is too hard to understand and endlessly alarms us? When history is continuously being rewritten revealing new truths? When it becomes difficult to distinguish what's real from what's not? Who are we? Where do we come from? Where are we going? What matters? It seems that our changing world has put personal, familial, community, national, and global identities into motion.

Additionally, in the year 2020, we witnessed the shock of a global pandemic and the havoc that it wreaked on how we experience life. Physical proximity became a fatal risk, and the emergence of social distancing and remote working further separated us from each other and possibly from our humanity. What happens when we live without hugs, kisses, high fives, fist bumps, and handshakes?

I believe this fundamental change in the human experience demands a new way of thinking about people and commerce. This change is in response to a metamorphosis of our world. Think of our world as changing from a caterpillar into a butterfly. Imagine what that might mean. All the basic rules are different. This metamorphosis is changing how people think, feel, behave, and their ability to act in the world. It presents a new set of challenges for businesses and organizations. Leaders are discovering that even as the role of technology increases, success depends on sensing and addressing the rapidly shifting values, expectations, and demands of people—the human side of business.

The metamorphosis of our world is profound. As our new world emerges and the old world falls away, there are big shifts in social, material, and mental domains:

- New technologies increase the amount and complexity of challenges and opportunities making the world difficult to understand and participate in.
- The exponential rate and intensity of change create unseen stresses on people and the need to continually adapt.
- Things don't always happen in a linear way which is confusing and produces un-expected outcomes. Causes and effects are not always sequentially bound together.
- Objects and people are changed by connection. In a world where everything is interconnected, this new flow of change makes it difficult to understand influences on thoughts and behavior.

New rules govern this new world. Instant change can come from surprising places. What really matters is often hidden where traditional leaders and problem solvers don't or can't look. The speed of networks often outstrips the velocity of decisions. Tiny forces can have immense impacts. It seems to be the age of the unthinkable. How do we adapt and effectively operate in this new environment? We need a new set of skills.

1

From Caterpillar
to Butterfly

THE NETWORKS AND SYSTEMS THAT DRIVE OUR DAILY LIFE have caused the emergence of a vastly new world. "The 21st century will be equivalent to 20,000 years of progress at today's rate of progress," says Ray Kurzweil, Google's director of engineering. "Organizations have to be able to redefine themselves at a faster sand faster pace."[2]

Over the next decade, we will experience massive social and cultural change, which will result in a complete overhaul of how we do business. When combining the dynamics of people and the internet—ubiquitous connected devices and systems, the dark web, alternate currencies, artificial intelligence (AI) with big data, global interconnectedness, ubiquitous computing, the digitization of matter, new modes of manufacturing (such as three-dimensional printing), and the sharing economy (with the barter and gifting economy)—it's easy to see how different the world is becoming. There will be persistent disruptions causing disequilibrium, increasing divergence and diffusion, shifts in power and ownership, virtual and augmented living, a significant automated workforce, and time compression.

The very nature of life as we know it is transforming before our eyes. The late German scholar Ulrich Beck, in his book *The Metamorphosis of the World: How Climate Change is Transforming Our Concept of the World,* explains that we are in an age of radical planetary and human change, change beyond revolution, and that

1

we are only at the beginning. Joshua Cooper Ramo, in his books *The Age of the Unthinkable: Why the New Global Order Constantly Surprises Us and What To Do About It and The Seventh Sense: Power, Fortune, and Survival in the Age of Networks,* talks about how the new dynamics of technocratic systems are fundamentally transforming humanity. I will touch on elements of the above ideas so that you gain insight into our new, changing world and do not risk seeing events and changes through an obsolete lens.

Recall all the unthinkable events you have observed such as 9/11, the financial crisis (for example, the failing global banking system), climate change, COVID-19 pandemic, ongoing mass shootings, global civil unrest in the face of entrenched income, racial and social inequality, a growing home-free population, personal gender transformation, and even the prospect of space tourism. With metamorphosis, old certainties of modern society fall away and something new begins to emerge. Metamorphosis alters our way of being in the world—the way we live in it, think about it, and seek to act upon it—and our chances of survival within it. As a sociological concept it refers to an unprecedented global change that involves two levels, the macro-level of the world and the micro-level of everyday human life.

It is important for you to be able to distinguish between a world decaying versus a world that is becoming something altogether different—and new. As Joshua Cooper Ramo writes in *The Seventh Sense,* "We live in a world that is both terribly exciting and awfully unsettling."[3] In our new, interconnected, networked world, old-style ideas lead us down dangerous paths. I encourage you to have a "new world" sensibility and not look to the past for answers. Don't focus on what has worked for others in another time, but on what can work for you moving into the future. It is not just the magnitude of change, but the speed of massive change, which is unnerving. As Beck states:

This all-encompassing, non-intentional, non-ideological metamorphosis that takes hold of people's daily lives is occurring almost inexorably, with an enormous acceleration that constantly outstrips existing possibilities of thought and action ... the metamorphosis of the world is taking place in world seconds with a speed that is nothing short of inconceivable, and as a result it is overrunning and overwhelming not just people but also institutions.[4]

I have found the most profound thinking about our time of epic change to be locked within heady academic texts, which hurt my hair to read. These are important ideas, so I'm going to share the highlights with you to help you connect the dots. If you like the ideas, you can dive deeper on your own. What's important is that the light bulb goes on about our changing world, so you'll be able to create the change you want to see in it.

VUCA

The acronym VUCA—volatile, uncertain, complex, ambiguous—was coined in 1987. It sprang from the leadership theories of Warren Bennis and Burt Nanus to describe general conditions and situations and was quickly adopted by the military. Eventually, VUCA made its way to becoming a trendy business managerial acronym as a way to understand our world.

I like to use VUCA as a term to cover the various dimensions of our new world:

- **Volatility:** The lack of predictability and the prospect for surprise. The more volatile the world is, the faster things change.

- **Uncertainty:** Connects with the above because of people's inability to understand what is going on, but also pertains to an environment in flux. The more uncertain the world is, the harder it is to predict what will happen next.
- **Complexity:** The myriad forces, the confusion of issues, no cause-and-effect chain. The more factors, the greater their variety, and the more they are interconnected, the more complex an environment is. The more complex the world is, the harder it is to analyze.
- **Ambiguity:** Lack of clarity about how to interpret something, haziness of reality, potential for misreads, the mixed meanings of conditions, and cause-and-effect confusion. A situation is ambiguous, for example, when information is incomplete, contradictory, or too inaccurate to draw clear conclusions from. The more ambiguous the world is, the harder it is to interpret.[5]

The four terms are, of course, interrelated. The more complex and volatile something is, the harder to predict and therefore more uncertain it will be. Yet, all four terms represent distinct elements that make our world harder to grasp and control. For most contemporary organizations, such as business, the military, education, and the government, VUCA pertains to the need to be aware and ready and deals with learning models for preparedness, anticipation, evolution, and intervention. It often relates to how people view the conditions under which they make decisions, plan forward, manage risks, foster change, and solve problems. In general, the premises of VUCA tend to shape an organization's capacity to:

- Anticipate the issues
- Understand the consequences of issues and actions

- Appreciate the interdependence of variables
- Prepare for alternative realities and challenges
- Interpret and address relevant opportunities

There are countless texts and graduate courses on VUCA, so please dig further if you like. I raise it here to make you aware of it, because it is a big idea that resonates with me, and it is a simple shorthand to underscore our new world, the new nature of problems, and the need for new kinds of ways to solve problems.

BACK TO BECK

In Beck's book, *The Metamorphosis of the World,* metamorphosis is a change in the fundamental worldview held by human beings and caused by the side effects of successful modernization such digital hyperconnectivity. Fixed certainties are not fixed anymore. For example, a nation is no longer the center of the world view around which all things revolve. It has been replaced by "the world" and "humanity" around which now all nations revolve. With climate change, for example, the world is not circulating around one nation, but nations are circulating around the world and humanity. Consider the internet. It communicates, but it also has the side effect of creating a connected humanity by connecting everyone with each other. People who have never left their villages, let alone ever boarded a plane, are closely and commonly linked with the world via their mobile phones. Beck sees these side-effects of modernization as driving the change and transforming the human experience: "In sum, metamorphosis is not social change, not transformation, not evolution, not revolution and not crisis. It is a mode of changing the nature of human existence."[6]

What is most important for our purposes, is that these radical shifts dissolve longstanding frames of reference and replace them with novel ones. Beck gives a historical example of reproductive medicine, which has caused a metamorphosis in motherhood, fatherhood, and parenthood. Throughout history, human reproduction in a lab was regarded as impossible, and the biological unity of mother and child was sacrosanct. That union, which historically marks the beginning of human life, was disrupted by medical technology. Although the old image of conception still dominates people's thinking, the reality is that what used to be intimate and almost sacred can now take place in a lab or a rented womb. As Beck states, "unintentionally, without a purpose, unawares, beyond politics and democracy, the anthropological foundations of the beginning of life are being reconfigured through the back door of the side effects of the success of reproductive medicine....Metamorphosis understood in this way as a global revolution of side effects."[7]

Beck aptly points out that we lag behind in our language and thoughts when facing this kind of novelty. Though we are often prisoners to traditional thinking and language as it preserves the old certainties and blinds us to new options, events such as the COVID-19 pandemic show that the right moment in history can lead to an explosion of new words and phrases to help us cope—"social distancing," "self-isolating," "covidiot," "work from home (WFH)," "quaranteams," "essential workers," "masking," and so on. Beck suggests, "Familiar concepts are becoming memory traces of a bygone era...Distinctions such as those between national and foreigners, nature and society, First and Third World, center and periphery don't seem to work. They are the writings on the wall of metamorphosis."[8]

In another example, Beck points to climate change as an agent of metamorphosis. It has altered our way of seeing the world and being in the world. Rising sea levels are creating new landscapes of inequality and redrawing world maps. Traditional images of humanity, which have been fixed for all time, are disintegrating while new ones are emerging. This injects us into not just new territory, but truly unknown territory.

The COVID-19 pandemic is what I think Beck would call an anthropological shock. This is when "many populations feel they have been subjected to horrendous events that leave indelible marks on their consciousness, will mark their memories forever, and will change their future in fundamental and irrevocable ways. Anthropological shocks provide a new way of being in the world, seeing the world and doing politics."[9] From this, social catharsis emerges including reflex, reflexivity, and reflections. The pandemic, climate risk, water shortage, and global civil unrest in the face of intolerable inequities signal new ways of being, looking, hearing, and acting in the world. Norms and imperatives that once guided decisions are now re-evaluated.

The last intriguing area of Beck's book that I'll mention is digital metamorphosis. According to Beck, while revolution is linear, progressive, intentional, and usually ideological, digital metamorphosis is the opposite. It is about the unintentional, often invisible side effects of modernization, particularly digital technologies, which have intertwined online and offline to change the human experience. When Steve Jobs introduced a new phone, he was changing how we were going to experience life.

Human experience is now highly digital and challenges traditional categories of existence such as status, social identity, collectivity, and individualization. For example, a person's status may no longer primarily be defined by their occupation, but, perhaps, by the number of online friends they have and the types of communities they are in. Social closeness has been decoupled from geography; fact, fiction, and reality are often blurred. In addition, as human beings we create oceans of data both consciously (use of social media, apps, and e-commerce) and unconsciously through everyday use of personal devices such as mobile phones and the surveillance systems built into modern environments such as swipe cards, electronic ticket kiosks, EZ tolls, and traffic lights. We can be tracked, probed, influenced and managed by the data we generate. Data exhaust is empowering and disturbing. It is how we allow machines to remove humanity from our lives.

"In the past we had punctuated evolution. Things changed abruptly and after the abrupt change, there were decades of stability. Every major technical or infrastructural shift asymptoted out moderately fast and then stayed fairly stable thereafter. Automobiles, canals, railroads. It is this stability that has enabled us to build really deep institutional models based upon these types of infrastructures and technologies thereafter. But maybe for the first time ever in the history of civilization we are entering a new techno-economic paradigm, a new type of infrastructure, a digital infrastructure that may just not asymptote out. It may just keep on going and going...Now of course infrastructure is more than just technologies. All serious infrastructures are social-technical paradigms and society and institutions have to fill in and respond."
— John Seely Brown, Chicago, May 2008[10]

THE UNTHINKABLE
AND SEVENTH SENSE: RAMO

One of the earliest people to identify this epochal change publicly and in an insightful way was Joshua Cooper Ramo, who opened my eyes with his book *The Age of the Unthinkable*.[11] His exploration uncovers the unique power of networks and the new counter-intuitive dynamics they create in the world. Like Beck, he questions how the unthinkable is happening over and over again. In *The Seventh Sense,* Ramo explores our hyperconnected world and discovers the great insight that "connection changes the nature of an object."[12] Ramo points us to Manuel Castells, the Spanish social philosopher, who states, "The network society represents a qualitative change in the human experience."[13]

Ramo works to help us grasp the nature of a new age and echoes much of what Beck says with a different perspective. Here are some ideas that opened my mind to seeing things differently:

- Network problems are unsolvable with traditional thinking.
- The speed of networks now outstrips the velocity of our decisions.
- We live in an era of connected crises where relationships now matter as much as any single object.
- Familiar borders like the ones dividing science and politics or military power and civilian safety begin to erode when everything is linked.
- There is a struggle between individual liberty and connection, because connection creates a "we."
- In modern networked systems, from stock exchanges to trade blocs, power is different. Tiny forces can have immense impacts.

- You cannot use a mechanical way of thinking in an age of complexity. You miss the energetic creative and destructive power of the complex connection.
- Many new challenges exhibit a worrying nonlinearity.
- Small forces produce massive effects. A few bad lines of code can paralyze an entire system.
- Crises cascade at a stunning scale.

EMERGENCE

Ramo does an outstanding job describing how most of our networked world is a pool of buzzing, fresh interaction—not only hard to predict but also constantly on the cusp of making something new. Scientists such as John Holland call this process "emergence," referring to the way that bottom-up interactions create a hybrid of form, idea, and thing that has never existed before.[14] This is a big idea you need to absorb, because "emergence" introduces unknown novelty. The idea that "emergence" happens by chance with no specific pattern is unnerving. It reminds me of the unintentional side effects of Beck.

As Peggy Holman, the author of *Engaging Emergence: Turning Upheaval into Opportunity* and a whole-systems consultant, explains: "In social systems, emergence can move us toward possibilities that serve enduring needs, intentions, and values. Forms can change, conserving essential truths while bringing forth innovations that weren't possible before. In journalism, traditional values of accuracy and transparency are making their way into the blogosphere, social network sites, and other emerging media."[15]

Networks are also responsible for what can be called the space-time compression. What is important for our purposes, is that people experience time differently. Time evaporates and accelerates. Think about what marks contemporary life: the sheer acceleration of life, the reduction of delay, and the emerging instant-ness of experience. There is also now a skill-time compression where technologies are able to place new, mind-shaping forces within instant reach (calling all *Matrix* fans).

Like Beck, Ramo finds language to be a stumbling block to embracing and building on novelty: "It's hard to let go of old notions, not just because we're attached to them, but because in many cases what we're being asked to hold on to next makes no sense to us."[16] This may be why the best companies, such as magazine publishers and Hollywood studios, struggle with a leap to the digital world. Ramo voices a concern about humanity in the world of technological networks. He says what will serve us best in a technological age is to strengthen and increase our sense of humanity, and to do the new thinking machines cannot match.[17]

Perspective on Enchantment

Larry Volpi is a creator of enchantment. A Madison Avenue advertising creator and brand maker, as well as a Hollywood screenwriter, over the decades Volpi has built iconic brands for the Marines and Kodak.

Jane: Why do you feel these times are so right for enchantment?

Larry: The whole world is going through this huge transformative change. We are all in the process of reassessing, revising, rethinking, recreating, recalibrating, redefining, restructuring—re, re, re, re. Also, we—America and the whole world—have become so numb. Not dumbed down but numbed down. We need to feel something. Enchantment unlocks and unleashes our humanness by tapping our imaginations.

Jane: What are people going through?

Larry: Today, there is so much incoming. Fake news. Alternative facts. So many rules and harsh reality must dos and what ifs. Our brains are overloaded. The upstairs hard drive is full. No space left. Everything is changing. Everything up for grabs. Our belief systems no longer work. But enchantment transcends all of that. A lot of things going on at present require a new filter, a new POV, a more human lens. Enchantment, if done right, opens a window to let the fresh air in so people can see and embrace the change, not fear or fall victim to it.

Jane: How does enchantment work?

Larry: It is a feeling, an emotion, and even a dream or memory that gets us out of our heads, and into ourselves. It enables us to go deeper within ourselves. And that's when it becomes heady. Enchantment taps our inner child. And you bet that kid wants to come out to play.

Jane: What does this mean for businesses?

Larry: The business world needs to become, in product, in environment, in essence, in communication of its own self—more human. As the grand maestro says, "Once more with feeling!" With enchantment, a feeling or memory or emotion can be translated to truly diverse—in age, culture, ethnicity, gender—groups and individuals. It speaks to them in a personal way. It is not a clever hard sell. It is not the engagement but the engaging that is crucial. Companies need to allow people to behold the wonder of the firefly, and not explain it away. Picture a war-weary battlefield, where from out of nowhere comes a butterfly. How unexpected? How magical? How mesmerizing? Caught up in its flight, how that butterfly holds and focuses our attention, bringing with it, some personal feeling and deeper meaning. This is the power and potential of enchantment.

TAKEAWAYS

- We live in a VUCA environment. This is not evolution or revolution, but metamorphosis of the world.
- The unintentional side-effects of modernity are driving metamorphosis, especially digital metamorphosis.
- The experience of being human is changing.
- The rate and magnitude of change are unprecedented, and there is no end in sight.
- Emergence and non-linear causes and effects are new dynamics at work.
- Small actions can cause massive outcomes in our hyperconnected, interdependent world.
- Language is often a barrier, holding back our understanding of possibilities.
- Imagination is key to humanity surviving and growing in this world.

QUESTIONS TO EXPLORE

- Everything is changed by connection. What does that mean to you?
- Imagine five unthinkable things that could change everything for your organization.
- How prepared is your organization for the new world?
- What idea did you find most surprising and why?

2
Unbridled Consumerism to New Essentialism

I
N THE UNITED STATES, WE LIVE TO BUY THINGS AND TO OWN
things. There's often a compulsive drive to possess more and
better things. We work hard to do this and even go into great
personal debt for it. The century-old saying "keeping up with the
Jones" seems quaint compared to our country's current relentless parade of Instagram-posts depicting luxury items, expensive
cars, and celebrity mansions. The internet boom and the constant
advance of new technologies such as the smartphone and AI have
pushed consumerism out of control.

In our society, we are convinced that possessions, spending,
and consuming are essential for happiness—and the more the
better. This is reinforced everyday across our culture. We are
exposed to an estimated 6,000 to 10,000 advertisements a day (up
from 500 to 1,600 in the 1970s)[18] and at least $244 billion in Ameri-
can and $560 billion worldwide is spent annually on advertising,[19]
often involving influential celebrities and people we admire that
tell us that buying a product or service will make our lives better
and even make us better: more attractive, smarter, or influential.
The building of this consumer culture occurred over decades and
pushed people into spending money they didn't have—all of this
was considered an acceptable practice.

Americans are drowning in debt. As a result of the 2008 financial crisis, many nest eggs cracked, forcing people into insolvency
and foreclosure. But in the more than ten years since, the ratio
between money earned versus money spent hasn't gotten much
better. According to the New York Federal Reserve, consumer
debt approached was $13.86 trillion after the second quarter of

2019—the twentieth consecutive quarter of an increase—up $219 billion from the previous quarter and up $1.2 trillion over the previous record high of $12.68 trillion in the third quarter of 2008. The consistent growth in debt has been in four main areas: home, auto, student loans, and credit cards. Credit-card loans crossed the $1 trillion mark, reaching $1.08-trillion in the third quarter of 2019 representing 26.2 percent of the total debt. The modern-day credit card—which arrived in the late 1950s—has led to financial disaster for many unbridled consumers and their families. According to the U.S. Census Bureau, more than 191 million Americans have a credit card, a charge card, or both. The average card holder has at least four cards and the average household with a card carries $8,398 in debt.[20] The average citizen is slaving to possess in a culture where they can never have enough and plunging them into toxic debt, which keeps them on a hamster wheel life of working and buying. The happiness they derive from owning excess physical possessions is fleeting at best and, at worst, deeply unsatisfying.

While unbridled consumption is destroying life for the average citizen, it is building trillion-dollar companies, creating the most billionaires ever on the planet, and driving a robust stock market. While some call this "income inequality," I see it as a feudalistic system that sucks the life out of modern-day peasants as they tirelessly work to support the fabulous, protected world of the wealthy. The numbers for the haves versus the have-nots in the United States, or rather the billionaires versus everyone else, became even more staggering during the coronavirus pandemic. According to CNN, American billionaires' fortunes rose $845 billion between March and August of 2020. That's right, Jeff Bezos, Bill Gates, Mark Zuckerberg and 640 of the wealthiest Americans saw their fortunes skyrocket while millions of Americans earned less than they were earning before the crisis began.[21] Not only do the rich always seem to get richer, it now seems that the poor have no protection against becoming poorer. More on just what the pandemic did to the consumer later on in this chapter.

One reason I am writing this book is because modern brands are partly responsible for this vicious cycle of excess consumption. Brands surround people twenty-four seven, and they penetrate the consciousness of a person, live in the memory and pop up all the time, often feeding on insecurities. You will be a real man if you shave with this razor brand. You are a great mom if you wash clothes with this detergent brand. You are part of the upper class if you wear this brand logo on your shirt. Brands operate on a deeply personal level, and most people are unaware of the constant brand influence. Beyond having these brands seared into our memories, they are reinforced every day as we are exposed to many brand promises at every turn, convincing us we can buy our identity (instead of being authentic) and happiness by owning branded possessions. Research suggests that buying branded material possessions doesn't deliver longstanding happiness and often creates unhappiness, stress, and anxiety, particularly if it involves accumulating debt. Yet, here we are, the greatest consumer culture of all time. Are we happy? According to the 2019 World Happiness Report, Finland remains the happiest country on earth while the U.S. fell from eighteenth to nineteenth place over the same period.[22]

Just to bring this home, the following illustrates the excessive consumption and unnecessary possession accumulation that brands have helped to create in America:

- Some reports indicate we consume twice as many material goods today as we did fifty years ago.[23]
- Americans spend $1.2 trillion annually on nonessential goods—in other words, items they do not need.[24]
- The U.S. has 5 percent of the world's population but consumes 30 percent of the world's resources.[25]

- The average size of the American home has nearly tripled over the past fifty years, while family size has remained the same.[26]
- One out of every ten Americans rents off-site storage—the fastest growing segment of the commercial real estate industry over the past four decades.[27] Personal storage in 2019 was $39 billion, nearly a 50 percent increase since 2010.[28]
- The average American woman owns thirty outfits—one for every day of the month. In 1930, that figure was nine,[29] and the average American throws away sixty-five pounds of clothing per year.[30]
- Women spend more than eight years of their lives shopping.[31]
- People work long and hard to pay bills, but still fall deeper into debt. In the fourth quarter of 2018, Americans added $26 billion in credit card debt, with one in ten people carrying $5,000 debt or more.[32]
- Almost half, 46 percent, of U.S. adults also say they have "an incredible" number of things that they could get rid of.[33]

Excessive material ownership is driven by brands that have us believing that possessing them will make us more secure, attractive, happy, convey our wealth and importance, and give us greater value in society. As a result, people spend their lives pursuing ownership of branded things that never really satisfy them. They can never really satisfy because they cannot actually answer the aching human need they trigger. We mistakenly look for confidence in the brand of clothes we wear or the brand of car we drive instead of actually developing the confidence. We look to overcome loss, loneliness, or heartache by purchasing branded things we don't really need, instead of actually addressing the issues.

CHAPTER 2

LIFE IN A FRENZY

In addition, modern consumerism is laced with a toxin—time compression. With the advent of time saving technologies, life has accelerated in the past ten years to an unbearable pace. Instantness has further undermined happiness. In fact, most people will tell you that life is too rushed, too hurried, and too stressed. We live at a feverish pace. Even children rush from one activity to another—often multitasking along the way. Overbooked, overstimulated, overwhelmed. We remain in constant connection with others through our phones, yet meaningful relationships still elude many. And it's a global phenomenon. The *Telegraph* reports that nearly half of all U.K. workers are too busy to leave their desks for lunch.[34] In order to get through our busy, multitasking-laden days, we consume a lot of coffee, energy drinks, energy bars, and other aids to help us gain more energy or better focus on the task at hand. We have a seemingly infinite marketplace with a dizzying array of branded products that we can buy with just a click. Life has been reduced to transactions, transactions that seem to happen ever quicker with less and less human connection.

I believe this frenzied pace and consumerism is partly responsible for the enormous increase in anxiety and despair. Anxiety disorders now affect 20 percent of Americans.[35] According to *The New York Times,* more teenagers than ever before are struggling with anxiety.[36] *U.S. News & World Report* reported that young adults in the eighteen to twenty-five age range reported more suicidal thoughts and bouts with depression from 2008 to 2010 than any other age group.[37] Xanax has seen a sharp rise in popularity with some experts saying it has become one of the top five drugs used by young people, alongside cannabis and alcohol. In 2017, Xanax was one of the most prescribed medication in the U.S. with 25 million prescriptions written.[38] The number of "deaths of despair"—a term coined in 2015 to describe fatalities caused by drug overdose, alcoholic liver disease, or suicide—have skyrocketed in the U.S. since 2000. In 2000, there were 22.7 deaths of despair per 100,000 Americans, a figure not that different from the 1970 rate of 21.5; by 2017, however, the rate doubled to 45.8 per 100,000.[39] Over the past three decades, deaths of despair among whites without a college degree have soared[40] and the suicide rate has risen steadily since the early 2000s, reaching 14.5 per 100,000 in 2017, the highest since 1938.[41]

One might argue that a culture that celebrates material possessions that are out of reach (and out-of-reach lifestyles and looks are often not real) and which provides faster, simpler ways for people to "click" into debt with brands that promise status and acceptance undermines the value of every human life. In truth, we are human beings and *not* what we consume. We are much more than that. When people are made to feel "less than" and come to believe it no matter what they buy or how hard they work, they fall into despair. This is the ugly side of consumerism. The struggle is real.

THE PANDEMIC THAT STOPPED THE WORLD

The above description of consumers, their compulsive spending, and their ever-increasing debt was B.P.—Before Pandemic. As things continued to spin out of control, an unexpected crisis changed everything. Everyone stopped. In almost an instant, people stopped going to work and worked from home. Children stopped going to school and learned from home. People stopped traveling. They stopped eating at restaurants and started cooking and eating at home. Instead of hiring people to do things, they did them themselves. They didn't go to stores and stopped buying lots of new things and started using the things they already owned. This change was forced upon them and it caused a metamorphosis.

This epic experience was shared globally. Everyone faced immediate and extended isolation, often from loved ones who were older or far away. Everyone faced uncertainty about what the pandemic was, what it would do, how to avoid it, what happened if they got it, what it would mean to their lives and when or if it would end. Everyone endured some form of loss—loss of freedom, many lost work and businesses, some lost friends and relatives to the disease. Everyone lost the life they were living. All families were home twenty-four seven. No going out to meet friends for a drink or dinner. No play dates for the kids or birthday parties. No going to the movies or to see a play or a concert. Everyone had to adapt to behaviors such as wearing a mask, social distancing, quarantining, washing hands, working from home, avoiding closed spaces including religious ceremonies and gyms, and eliminating mass gatherings such as sporting events, concerts, and theaters.

Some left their homes and quarantined with family to reduce living costs, to escape urban centers; others moved to the suburbs or took advantage of working remotely and relocated their primary residence to resort towns such as Aspen and Key West, micropolitan cities such as Taos, New Mexico and second-tier cities like Jacksonville, Florida and Raleigh, North Carolina. Work-from-home percentages in the double digits were almost exclusively in small towns and suburbs, where real estate has boomed. There was a lot of movement. About one out of five Americans moved due to COVID-19 or knows someone who did, and 52 percent of young adults moved in with their parents—a new high.

Everyone picked up a new vocabulary which includes such terms as lockdown, quarantine, "essential workers," "flattening the curve," and "covidiots." We all listened to confusing news reports about what the virus was, where it came from, how it spread and what to do to prevent it. Most of all—as we radically changed our routines and our life—we also thought long and hard. As a result, something deep inside was awakened and grew. Maybe it was survival instinct that sparked it, but something very unusual began to happen. In the midst of a life-threatening pandemic, people started to relax, slow down, let go, open up, and feel more. They began to experience more of their humanity and moments of real happiness.

The sudden, intense, prolonged pandemic experience led to four big transformations:

- ***The introduction of excess time.*** People who were not essential workers began to experience time differently. They often had more of it and more control over it. Time slowed down. They started to experience the true length of a day—it's long—and realized there was time to do lots of things. They began to value time differently, to see how they were wasting time by not more fully experiencing it. They started to use time differently. This gift of time was radically new to them, and they began to use it in ways that gave them pleasure and that did *not* include the massive buying of possessions. In fact, personal spending went down and savings went up. A miracle.

- ***People had time to think.*** People had so much time, they began to think. Even people who never took a moment to think, couldn't help it. It was irrepressible. They began to think about things they never thought about. The more they thought, the more their thoughts grew and grew. This led to new realizations and ideas. They started to see the world in a more personal way, through their own eyes. They stepped out of the frenzied consumerism and into their personal world. Living twenty-four seven in their own homes, surrounded by family and loved ones, pets, plants, nature, music and things they selected. It was a cocoon. They started to see and to think about their possessions. There were so many. They wondered whether they needed all of these possessions, and if they needed such a crazy life with such a crazy pace in order to buy more of them. The pandemic forced them to discover the joy of simplicity—slower pace, being home (one place), having time—and having lots of new "things" was not a part of this joy. Imagine that. Joy not related to material possessions and the experience of spending. Something deep inside started to change.

- *The freedom to do.* With the gift of time, also came the freedom to use it. People took the excess time and started to do things with it that they always wanted to do. There was a surge in learning and doing fun things. How many people do you know that started to learn something new during the pandemic? Learning to play a musical instrument, paint, cook, raise chickens, grow vegetables, write, build, and more. Many sought greater self-reliance and picked up how-to skills for doing things around their home. Many jumped into play, playing old board games, picking up a tennis racket, a basketball, or a puzzle. Some discovered nature and walking became a new daily activity rather than running on a treadmill in the gym. Pickleball exploded as a new activity. There were lots of new and shared experiences in the close quarters at home. People took the time not to work more or buy more, but to do things they enjoyed more. The joy they experienced inspired them to explore more and to discover new things that intrigued them. Happiness blossomed. And this was authentic enjoyment that came from a desire within. It just happened organically as they reacted to the pandemic.

- *A change in relationships.* The pandemic cut people off from people and restricted contact to the same very few—the family, the pod. As people began to spend lots of time with very few people, things changed and relationships happened. Parents, fathers in particular, began to spend lots of time with their children. The "family" began to experience what it meant to be a family in deeper ways, because family time was twenty-four seven. Couples experienced greater depth from constantly being together—the good and the bad. Relationships grew due to constant, isolated proximity. The pandemic also separated people from all kinds of people such as co-workers, distant friends, relatives, and service people. This led people to think more about the people who did and did not matter to them, and some were surprised by the people they actually missed. People experienced longing, heartache, and pining for human connection and began to realize the importance of spending time with people they cared for and who cared about them.

All of this change led people to realize what was essential to them, not in pragmatic terms but in happiness terms, in deeply human, personal terms. Within a mandated simple, isolated, personal world, people blossomed in an unexpected way.

THE PANDEMIC COCOON

During the pandemic, many people ironically started to feel better despite the fear, uncertainty, loss, and change. They were surrounded mostly by things and people they enjoyed—and that changed them. The pandemic helped humanity shed the old skin of established routines. The pandemic unleashed realizations about what really mattered and that led to different choices and new ways of thinking about life. What emerged was a consciousness aligned with a world in metamorphosis—uncertain, unexpected, uncharted. No one was planning on this personal transformation. It wasn't part of a self-help or anti-consumerism effort. It grew organically from within.

Due to the prolonged nature of the pandemic, this transformation was not fleeting. The thoughts and experiences had time to grow, take root, and evolve. People created new habits and new structures. Home Depot's business boomed as people started transforming their homes into multi-use spaces: an office, a classroom, a gym, an art studio, and, of course, a real home. They adopted Zoom and other online meeting tools to conduct business and stay close to those they couldn't see who lived far away. A hope for permanent Work From Home (WFH) turned into a reality for some (for instance, employees at Twitter, Facebook)[42] and a growing desire for most. Economists at Harvard Business School predict that when the pandemic is over, one in six workers will continue working from home or co-working two days a week.[43] Another survey of hiring managers by the global freelancing platform Upwork found that one-fifth of the workforce could be entirely remote after the pandemic.

Many employees let their hair grow long, go gray; pandemic beards were common. Many began new routines that included morning walks, preparing meals with care (instead of rushing to throw dinner on the table), family hikes, and biking. Sales of bikes, kayaks, boats, scooters, and other equipment for outdoor activities boomed. Drive-in movies came back. People were taking time to have a new kind of fun. As months passed, new routines became a new way of life and quietly ignited internal growth.

At least half of Americans created pods, small groups largely of family and neighbors, with whom they could safely socialize and have close contact. Robert J. Waldinger, an American psychiatrist and professor at Harvard Medical School best known for directing the world's longest-running longitudinal study tracking health and mental well-being, learned that relationships hold the key to happiness.[44] Close relationships—more than money or fame—help delay mental and physical decline and are better predictors of long and happy lives than social class, IQ, or even genes. The pandemic led to closer relationships.

One thing that did not boom during the pandemic was purchases of material goods, especially non-essential material goods such as luxury goods, clothes, and jewelry. Big, well-established retailers such as Lord & Taylor, Sur la Table, The Paper Store, Brooks Brothers, Lucky Brand, J.C. Penney, Neiman Marcus, J.Crew, True Religion, and Pier 1 all declared bankruptcy.[45] The rate of personal savings hit a historic high of 33 percent in April 2020 and spending declined by a record 13.6 percent.[46] Unemployment hit record highs, stores had limited hours and inventory. People also had less need. They were stuck at home. Various factors created a realization about stuff. People started to realize what they didn't need—and with delight. They did not miss continually acquiring things and the experience of constant spending. I never heard a single person complain of shopping withdrawal, quite the opposite. People seemed to love doing other things.

People had epiphanies related to consumption during this time. They began to understand the costs of having excess stuff and unnecessary things. They realized that a demanding work life, which was required to support their high consumption, had been taking a lot of life's time, creating high stress, and zapping personal energy. Did they need to work that hard? Was it worth it? In addition, they also realized it was much easier, less stressful, and less costly to live with less stuff. They started to see how they could change their lives for the better.

Consumption during the pandemic contracted and also shifted. People were still spending, albeit less, but differently. They were more thoughtful in what they spent their money on, making sure the expense was worth it in the new world. For example, they shifted consumption away from things that gave them social status to activities that gave them personal joy, such as outdoor sporting experiences and adventures, fun tasks and games, art and entertainment, having pets, and re-shaping their personal nests. Those that could afford it even purchased new real estate to create family compounds and weekend retreats. This spending was not about finding belonging, escaping, or keeping up with the Joneses. It was about enjoying life according to personal activities and life with others. Surprisingly, it was so simple.

As people had time to think during the pandemic, they also became acutely aware of social injustices. It was like dust being visible in the light. Activism blossomed. The Black Lives Matter movement became a global rallying cry for ending systemic racism and implicit bias. People took to the streets all over world and in America even the smallest of towns had protests. Despite political leaders' indifference, citizens felt their agency in the world and took action. Police forces came under scrutiny with a mandate for reform, better training, and accountability. Diversity and inclusion was no longer an ideal; rather, they became an immediate imperative for a new reality. Hiring practices were challenged, and people started calling others out on racist behavior. In addition, with "cancel culture," people used their consumer power as a weapon for social change.

People started to become conscious of the changes they were making. They talked about these changes with joy: how they were no longer going to overextend at work or socially and no longer going to over-consume in their life. They intended to simplify, drastically, not subtly adjust. They were enjoying a new way of life, which was changing them for the better and wanted it to continue. Just like that, the hamster wheel of the greatest consumer culture in the history of humankind stopped and was disassembled.

THE RISE OF NEW ESSENTIALISM

The pandemic issued a global invitation to slow down, consume less, and enjoy more. People accepted. In doing so, they experienced more control, freedom, intentionality, and personal passion. Many started to realize they had been chasing after the wrong things. People became more aware of their interests and more active in pursuing them and developing their abilities. They experienced greater openness, curiosity, awe, wonder, love, moments of joy and peace, new possibilities and depth of relationships. They discovered they could accomplish things, that they had agency in the world. These discoveries combined with the sustained liberation from the frenzied consumer culture gave birth to new worldview that is growing and changing the nature of modern humanity. I call it the "new essentialism." It is not about sacrificing. In fact, it is the opposite of sacrifice even though it means ownership of far fewer things. It is about realizing and grasping for things that really matter for personal happiness. It is almost effortless, because it authentically comes from within, from a deep self that has been awakened and opened by the pandemic experience.

A new consciousness gave rise to the new essentialism because many people experienced:

- Freedom from the passion to possess
- Freedom from the feverish mania of modern life
- Freedom to discover who they really are, what they really like
- Freedom to be in relationships, not on the edge of relationships

The new essentialism removes much of the frivolous and insignificant and adds greater meaning and value to the life experience.

It is freedom from the modern hysteria to live faster and delivers power in keeping just essentials. It is marked by five traits:

- *Joyful frugality:* Indulging in essentials that bring personal joy.
- *Self-renaissance:* Awakening of deep personal wants and taking actions to fulfill them, increasing discovery and clarity of likes and pursuing experience to enjoying them.
- *Mindful accountability:* Highlighting our human interdependence. Persistent protests, sometimes violent, kept social injustice top of mind. From forest fires in the West to tropical storms in the South, the destructive effects of climate change felt real. During the pandemic downtime, people started thinking more about what they could do to help and embraced changing their consumption. Repurpose, re-use, re-cycle. They sought out companies that aligned with their values and veered away from buying from companies with unethical business practices.
- *Self-reliance:* Preference for do-it-myself, rely on my own skills which also means to keep things simpler and more-doable until skills can develop. Reflected in dramatic rise in online skills learning from many places including Masterclass, Coursera, Skillshare, and universities. The ed tech industry was a $107 billion market in 2015 and is expected to triple by 2025 to $350 billion.[47] Build your own furniture, make your own meals, cut your own wood, cut your husband's hair, groom your own pets, and so on. Gives a sense of control and readiness for whatever might come.

MINIMALISM MEETS INDULGENCE

New essentialism feels life-giving and life-freeing and builds on the countercultural movement of "minimalism," which had traction before the pandemic. In 2018, an estimated 10 percent of Americans said they already considered themselves to be minimalists, and one in four said the either wanted to become a minimalist one day or were actively working towards it.[48] Minimalism is philosophically about removing the distraction of excess possessions in order to allow focus on things that matter most and runs contrary to a consumer culture built on accumulating possessions. Minimalists live free from the all-consuming passion to possess and seek happiness elsewhere such as in relationships, experiences, and soul-care. It's about "Own less. Live More. Discover the Life You Want."

New essentialism achieves many of the same outcomes of minimalism but comes from a different place. It is not done out of sacrifice or righteousness. The choices emerge from indulging in authentic living and personal choices that bring pleasure. New essentialists are on a path that is growing and evolving. The new essentialism experience features:

- Life slowed down
- More time, time experienced more fully
- Removing the frivolous and keeping the significant
- Spending less, consuming less
- De-cluttering and creating more space
- Minimal time spent on maintenance of things
- Liberation from having less stuff
- Deeper relationships with a close few
- Environmentally friendly and sustainable living practices
- Self-reliance and do-it-myself
- Increased productivity from ability to be more focused and efficient at tasks
- Being examples that their children can follow
- Taking better care of what they own

- Exploring to discover what they like and doing more of it
- Taking time for rest, boredom, naps, daydreaming

New essentialism changes the context for brands. Simplicity is now a cornerstone of a life well lived, which means having less is really more. This fundamentally challenges consumerism. Therefore, promoting excess consumption no longer resonates. Second, identity, growth, and happiness are not dependent on brand consumption, but on authentic personal choices related to non-material things such as learning, skills, love, environment, and relationships. Third, people are intolerant of practices that violate their values, so brands must be sensitive, empathetic, and align accordingly. Last, people are concerned about exhaustive work commitments that steal from and sacrifice the pursuit of life's happiness and build the wealth of the few at the expense of the many. They want more control and more balance and meaning from their work, which I believe will manifest into new labor demands and a new American work ethos. Brands will need to play a role in helping companies forge real human commitment with employees, customers, vendors, investors, and the public at large.

ENCHANTED BRANDS MEET THE NEW ESSENTIALISM

With the ethos of mass consumption waning and new essentialism rising, people need new cultural symbols—Enchanted Brands—that reflect and speak to the deep-seated need for authenticity in a world that threatens to reduce the quality of the human experience. They no longer need brands that sell by promising identity or belonging. They need brands that serve their fresh approach to life and help them grow in the face of novelty, complexity, and uncertainty. Brands that give them power, bring stability, comfort, faith, confidence, and build emotional strength. Brands in the twentieth century sold stuff, because consumerism (buying things) was the answer to achieving happiness. Enchanted Brands in the twenty-first century serve people, because helping people use their imagination to embrace newness and their humanity (and not let technology make them act more like a machine) is the answer to achieving happiness in an increasingly dehumanizing world.

New essentialism is a true renaissance as people rise up and live how they want to live and act to change the world into what they want it to be. This includes ending exploitation of people, being mindful of and accountable for consequences to humanity, and making sure institutions (which cannot be trusted) do what is best for people—the human side of business. Enchanted Brands are an important pivot for companies, as they are visible cues that a company is aligned to help build a better world. Enchanted Brands change the structure of the brand relationship from consumption based (buy this) to empowerment based (use this to do something). They don't sell a specific future for you to buy (closed), rather they promise the possibility for you to create the future you want (open). They feed the imagination to allow people to envision, they share the standards and values demanded by people, and they provide the mind nourishment people need to be strong. These brands are not celebrities to be worshipped. They are coveted power tools that individually and collectively arm humanity, whether they are purchased or not, with the ability to do more and enjoy more of what it means to be human.

CHAPTER 2

Perspective on Happy Money

Dr. Elizabeth Dunn is a happiness expert and a professor in the Department of Psychology at the University of British Columbia and co-author, with Dr. Michael Norton, of Happy Money: The Science of Happier Spending (Simon & Schuster).

Jane: You conduct research that looks at the relationship between spending and happiness. What kind of spending makes sad money?

Elizabeth: Debt is quintessential sad money. We've done research that shows that debt can be pretty toxic in the context of marital relationships.

Jane: What's the key to getting more happiness from our spending?

Elizabeth: If you're going to go into debt, it's definitely not worth it. It's so hard for just about anything you buy to provide you with enough happiness to offset the happiness costs of going into debt. When I say debt, I mean the kind of credit card debt that hangs over people's heads, that fills them with a sense of dread. If you're spending all of your time working so that you can afford your Tesla, or not going out to dinner with friends because you've put all this money into fancy furniture for your house, it's not worth it. It's really about the trade-offs that come into play.

Jane: How do people know what kind of expenditures make them happy?

Elizabeth: It's not necessarily easy to figure out what does and doesn't make us happy. I buy this V-neck sweater from the Gap. I think it's a good idea. I end up not really wearing it. I give it away a year later. It never really makes me happy. At what point do I go, maybe material things aren't that great and would I be better off spending on experiences? That's a big mental leap people need to make.

Jane: What kind of spending delivers the most happiness?

Elizabeth: I would say charitable giving and buying experiences that don't create debt. If you're going to have an awesome experience, see if you can pay for it first so you don't have the prospect of having to pay for it later hanging over your head and detracting from your positive experience. The euphoric end is probably more of the buying experience itself and maybe the really high-impact charitable gift. But euphoria isn't everything. Just being able to breathe and feel like your life isn't spinning out of control also has a lot of value.

Jane: What shifts have you seen in spending?

Elizabeth: One of the really clear shifts is in more experiential purchases over material purchases. It was around 2005 or 2006 when my colleagues published their first work showing that buying experiences provides more happiness than buying material things. I've also seen, more and more companies with the leaders saying, I'm not satisfied with just making money. I actually want our company to have a mission and something that we really care about.

Jane: Did the pandemic experience help people realize anything about their spending?

Elizabeth: To figure out what makes us happy, it's really helpful if we can experiment on ourselves. As terrible as the pandemic has been for so many people, it has provided this opportunity to experiment with different approaches to daily life. I have a friend who's a lawyer, makes a good income. She's just found herself shopping so much less throughout the pandemic. She was like, oh, I don't miss it. She would've always assumed that having pretty new clothes and all these things were important for her happiness, but then when she gave them up, it didn't matter.

Jane: What would it take to help people have happier money?

Elizabeth: It's so easy to fall into this trap of habitual spending that really builds up this cycle of debt. We need to shift the whole cultural conversation. If I could get people to pause and ask themselves, will this purchase really make me happy and can I learn from my past experience? I think that can reduce spending and result in greater well-being for a whole lot of people.

TAKEAWAYS

- Unbridled consumerism promoted excess material possessions that often left consumers in debt and despair.
- The great American consumer culture is over forever, shattered by lifestyle disruption of the pandemic, which opened minds to a new way of life.
- Moving forward, people will be less defined by what they own and continue to see identity outside of material possessions.
- People will consume less, own less, and enjoy a lightness of being in breaking free from the frenzied materialism of the twentieth century.
- New essentialism is a global consciousness rising from the pandemic cocoon where minimalism meets self-indulgence in a true renaissance of personal authenticity.
- An increased sensitivity to social justice is part of the new essentialism with people taking anti-consumer action against brands and companies whose actions do not create a better world.
- A new kind of brand is needed in this new era, one that serves rather than sells, because the answer to happiness no longer lies in simply owning material goods. New brands must give people more agency in the world. They must also act as the cultural cues of humanity's strength.

QUESTIONS TO EXPLORE

- What are all the ways that new essentialism might affect your business?
- With people buying less, how can you earn more and create more value?
- What aspects of new essentialism might represent growth opportunities?
- How might new essentialism affect the mindset and work ethos of your employees, partners, and vendors?
- How can your brand shift to align with the new essentialism and serve rather than sell to people?
- How is your organization helping to create a better world?

3

The Search for New Coherence: The Struggle to Understand the Unthinkable Effects of Metamorphosis

AS THE WORLD IS IN METAMORPHOSIS AND NEW ESSENTIAL-ism is transforming consumerism, there is another dynamic that changes the landscape of how we connect with people. I call it the search for new coherence. Simply put, the world is too complex for people to understand; this is an untenable state and people are adopting ways of dealing with it which may have dramatic effects for your organization. There is more resistance, scrutiny, and in some cases outright rebellion to the forceful projection of views by brands and companies. In addition, there is a rise in people making up their own version of the truth to influence actions.

In the 2018 book *Truth Decay*, by leaders of the RAND Corporation, we learn about the grand challenge facing modern society related to the weakening of understood truth.[50] The four dimensions of truth decay are:

- Increasing disagreement about facts and analytical interpretations of facts and data
- A blurring of the line between opinion and fact
- Increasing relative volume influence of opinion and personal experience over fact
- Declining trust in formerly respected sources of factual information.

One way to approach these challenges is to accept that truth and fact are no longer absolute for people anymore. To bring people together around a common understanding of anything, we need more than fact as facts are increasingly unstable and contradictory. We can't simply disseminate facts in a clever or entertaining way, as in the past, because it no longer works. We must also generate trust, faith, and desire along with the facts if we are to complete the puzzle of acceptance, and that acceptance can only come from one credible place—personal discovery.

I am exploring the search for new coherence with you now, because the more you understand about this driving need, the better you will be able to address the risks and opportunities of it with customers, employees, investors, and the general public. Remember that when people need to understand something beyond their comprehension, facts alone won't cut it. It requires a leap of faith, trust, and desire to believe—all of which you can create with your Enchanted Brand.

THAT NEW PATH TO
ACCEPTED UNDERSTANDING

People ache for relief from the unrelenting onslaught of disorienting change. Historically, when people could not understand the world around them, they turned to myth. Today, we see a surge in conspiracy theories, so-called fake news, and mysticism as people search for answers. The search for new coherence disrupts how people have traditionally processed information and accepted truth. As leaders, we must help people find their truth—truth in why they invest in, work for, partner with, buy from, and support your organization.

I believe people are increasingly aware that there is not one truth, but many. This uncomfortable realization is settling in and has implications for how we connect with people. Truth is personal and subjective. It depends on your perspective. With our recent enlightenment on ethnic diversity, we have come to more clearly understand how perspectives vary greatly and how flawed many of our historical, cultural, and political narratives have been. This realization alters a long tradition of how we create a consensus of mind.

We have seen how people resist someone else's truth being forced upon them with the rise in activism from consumers, citizens, and even board members. If you give people a truth (your version of a truth), they will question it, scrutinize it, may work to discredit it, and will most likely discard it. Acceptance is unlikely. Why? Because in today's upside-down world, people can only trust themselves. Rather than give them the truth, you must help them to discover it on their own. That's a lot harder and a real paradigm shift for marketing and even leadership. Resist the temptation to give all the answers. Allow people to find the answers. This is counter to traditional marketing and branding practices which are prescriptive and directive and no longer work. The fastest way to an accepted truth today is not a direct path.

Facts and ideas need to be interpreted and personally processed before they become accepted. Facts alone are insufficient to make a personal truth, because we never have 100 percent of the facts. Plus, facts do change and often contradict each other. It is hard to rely on the facts or even believe in them. Therefore, we need to surround the facts with three things. One, trust in the facts and source of the facts—real and credible. Two, belief in the possibilities of what the facts suggest—plausible. Three, a desire to accept what they mean even if you cannot entirely understand—I want this to be true. Together, this brings the leap of faith needed for acceptance. So, how are we able to achieve a common understanding across diverse populations and perspectives if we are not being direct and prescriptive? By stimulating the imagination in a very specific way, people will generally arrive in the same place. This is best explained by digging around in the power of myth.

THE UNIQUE POWER OF MYTH

Myth has existed in every society and is a basic constituent of human behavior. For thousands of years when people could not make sense of the world around them, they created myths to help fill in the gaps—fables, fairy tales, folktales, legends. What is fascinating about a myth is that it is neither completely true nor completely false. That may be why they persist. Myths attempt to make sense of our perceptions and feelings within our experience of the world. They refer to very real human experiences, which is why they resonate. In a culture where the abstract theories of academics are out of touch and often feel meaningless, myths communicate more effectively and more universally.

In a scientific world, myth is often viewed as valueless cultural artifact. Several academics at the turn of the twentieth century (most notably Englishman E.B. Tylor, German Max Müller, and Scottish social anthropologist James Frazer) proclaimed myths to be worthless and characterized them as failed attempts at science. What these reductionist theorists failed to understand was the deeper significance and function of myth within the human psyche. It was the Swiss psychiatrist and psychoanalyst Carl Jung who suggested that mythical stories connected individuals and societies with the "collective unconscious" in which all humans partake, and were one way that humanity interacted with the vast unseen world.[51] Romanian thinker Mircea Eliade went further and suggested that myth helped individuals know how to make sense of their world and behave in society. Academic Joseph Campbell built on the work of Jung to argue that myth has an important function in society in four ways: It evokes a sense of awe, it supports a religious cosmology, it supports a social order, and it introduces individuals to the spiritual path of enlightenment. Campbell's work significantly influenced filmmaker George Lucas, who said he wanted the *Star Wars* films to be a "myth for modern man."[52] Campbell also influenced Christopher Vogler, a script doctor for Disney studios, whose work *The Writer's Journey: Mythic Structure for Writers* is a central text in Hollywood.[53] Dozens of movies followed Vogler's mythic structure for plot and characterization and brought myth alive today. Modern myth-making through movies has become a cultural tsunami that the brains of the early twentieth century could never have imagined.

In popular culture, myth connects our global society as it is a universal language. Luke Skywalker, Frodo Baggins, Spider-Man, and Batman transcend cultural divides. Mythic heroes communicate universal values in their fight against evil. People share vicariously in the hero's quest and experience a cathartic transformation. They follow the hero through moral choices and realize (even unconsciously) that they live in a moral universe. They come to understand that there is not only a plot and meaning to the story, but there is a plot and meaning to life. Writers J. R. R. Tolkien [54] and C. S. Lewis were each fascinated with the power of myth. Tolkien intentionally devised *The Lord of the Rings* as a myth for the English people, to replace the Arthurian cycle.

"There are only two worlds—your world, which is the real world, and other worlds, the fantasy. Worlds like this are worlds of the human imagination: their reality, or lack of reality, is not important. What is important is that they are there. These worlds provide an alternative. Provide an escape. Provide a threat. Provide a dream, and power; provide refuge, and pain. They give your world meaning."
— **Neil Gaiman, author**[55]

MODERN CONSPIRACY THEORY

In May 2020, *The Atlantic* put out an entire "Conspiracy Theory" issue.[56] Adrienne LaFrance's cover story argues that the QAnon-inspired belief that Donald Trump is locked in a secret war with a deep state cabal of child molesters is on its way to becoming something like a religion. Welcome to world of modern conspiracy theory. Some people dabble in it for amusement as it connects them to other people in their circles and gives a sense of agency or fate. For others, it serves as a coping mechanism. Some say the myths we see moving people today are nothing compared to those that we will have to take seriously in the times to come. Buckle your seatbelt.

This spike in conspiracy is a form of mythmaking. Marxist literary theorist Fredric Jameson explores conspiracy narrative in his 1992 book *The Geopolitical Aesthetic*.[57] He proposes that high-tech, globalized capitalism has made the world more and more difficult for the average person to comprehend using inherited explanations and traditional symbols. The leaps of logic in conspiracy are an attempt to find a concrete narrative for a world that has grown too complex to wrap one's head around. Conspiracy makes an inscrutable world seem knowable. Instead of being adrift in a shifting sea of random, mysterious images and events, you have a master signifier of a plot that gives meaning to it all—and a corresponding sense of subjective power (of being able to interpret the world) and intellectual purpose (of teaching others that knowledge). Conspiracy thinking involves leaps of imagination—and for that reason it makes life seem, not just righteous and meaningful, but also exciting. This thrill is clearly part of its appeal.

The natural activity of grouping together elements to form a picture is how a conspiracist connects the dots to find the secret plot that makes a satisfying pattern of a disordered reality. Interestingly, the theories tend to be likelier to thrive if they are elaborate and outlandish, rather than simple and logical. For this reason, they are very nearly impervious to mockery, and constantly cross over from fiction to reality in a way that can be hard to keep track of, let alone argue with.

Conspiracy is flamboyant and colorful and involves leaps of imagination. One of the earliest internet-era conspiracy theories, "Ong's Hat" (look it up) also began as an online art project by Joseph Matheny.[58] It took on an eerie life of its own, and despite Matheny's later protestations that the project was born as an attempt at culture jamming (hoaxing the media so as to make people second-guess the narratives they are consuming), there are those who still believe this is all part of the cover-up of a secret world of parallel dimensions.

Conspiracy clearly has the appeal of being in on a secret language, of finding symbolic community with others. Critic and art historian Eleanor Heartney recently explained the surging appeal of magical art (art connected to the occult and mysticism) with factors that are similar to the appeal of conspiracy theory. Heartney says that a generalized sense of hopelessness about the social order leads people to hunt for new narratives of empowerment. She talks about a feeling of encroaching chaos that amplifies the appeal of alternative codes of meaning to give an order to it all; a disenchantment with soulless commercial culture that leaves people looking to attach themselves to the romance of secret knowledges.[59]

DEMAND FOR ENCHANTED BRANDS

Enchanted Brands fill the void that myth, conspiracies, and magical art also fill. They provide a context that gives coherence and meaning in a world where both are in high demand. At a time when we are suffering from an absence of understanding and there seems to be a sudden plunge into darkness that leaves massive numbers of people looking for any light to guide them to safety, Enchanted Brands can bring the light. These brands can provide a graspable narrative to help people navigate a painful reality and a world that doesn't seem to make sense.

Clearly, some level of myth is needed to help people achieve understanding. Since the beginning of time, people have used their imaginations to fill in the gaps for truth. From Greek gods to myths and legends across cultures, people have unified behind ideas that gave coherence. This required the use of the imagination, belief, and desire. As people search for new coherence, Enchanted Brands can disarm the fear, open the mind, and reduce the struggle by helping people explore scenarios in their own mind. Unlike wild conspiracy theories, which often emanate from unknown or opaque sources, Enchanted Brands are accountable societal custodians with clear owners and transparent objectives.

The desperate search for new coherence is dangerous and increasing. Some will seize it for nefarious purposes or private agendas. I believe Enchanted Brands can meet the new coherence need and offer a satisfying alternative to conspiracy narratives. Enchanted Brands can open imaginations to get people feeling more comfortable with multiple truths and unthinkable possibilities. Like works of art, Enchanted Brands help people to think and imagine on their own. In doing so, they allow people to come to a deeper reflection and understanding and become more capable of action. The key is not to provide the answer but to empower people to find their own. This is the task of an Enchanted Brand. Indeed, exercising the imagination may very well be the ticket to sanity in an insane world. Minimally, it should create comfort amidst chaos.

On a macro, cultural level these brands can become building blocks of transforming human experience and connective tissue in a changing social culture by making the unknowable, knowable; the complex, simple; the novel, familiar; and the scary new into exciting new. People are longing for compelling coherence and Enchanted Brands can become ubiquitous stimulators on the cultural landscape to cultivate new understandings. By amplifying imaginative possibilities, they help people know that just because you don't understand everything, doesn't mean you can't have agency in the world.

TAKEAWAYS

- Our world has become too complex for people to understand, causing a hunger search for understanding.
- Facts no longer provide sufficient answers as they are incomplete and often unreliable.
- Truth is no longer absolute, but personal. There are many truths related to a single item.
- To achieve consensus of mind, we must take a new approach that facilitates personal discovery.
- Personal truth requires facts, trust, faith, and desire.
- The search for new coherence is a vulnerability and opportunity.
- Enchanted Brands meet the need for new coherence by strengthening the imagination.

QUESTIONS TO EXPLORE

- What is too complex to understand about your organization for employees, customers, investors, partners, and the public?
- How do you fight the emergence of fake news, false understandings, or destructive gossip?
- What are some kinds of conspiracy theories that could emerge?
- Which myths, if any, can you draw upon for your brand?
- How can you change your approach to help people to discover the truth you want them to know?

4

The Human Side of Business: People Must Come First

I N A VUCA WORLD, IT IS NOT BUSINESS AS USUAL. EVEN THOUGH we live in a technological, increasingly automated world, people have become the X factor. More than ever, people are the single factor determining the fate of your organization and they are taking back control of their lives.

For years, people were marginalized at the expense of profits. The human side of business suffered while bottom lines flourished. Now, at this time of epochal change, people are more sensitized, aware, volatile, and unpredictable. They cannot be controlled or coerced using traditional means. Think of activist environmentalist investors pulling the rug out from under Exxon, and the Reddit rogues democratizing stock market participation and bringing institutional investors to their knees. People are taking control in wildly unexpected ways.

Activist investors have become a new way of life and have tossed out CEOs and redirected companies. The so-called "cancel culture" has shown how the general public will tar and feather, abandon, and take down a brand they feel does not support making the world a better place in one form or another. People are increasingly taking action to create the change they want to see in the world.

One sacred cow is already getting slaughtered. In the wake of a long era where maximizing shareholder value reigned as an almost inalienable driving principle of business even as it compromised and marginalized people in its pursuit, there is an almost explosive cultural sensibility that will no longer tolerate profits over people. The human cost is too high. The exploitation of human capital for the excessive personal gain of the few, popularized as income inequality, is no longer sustainable. Perhaps we can reach for value-based profits, where revenues and social good are intertwined.

In addition, we already examined how people are choosing to consume less and pursue happiness in ways that exist largely outside of the market, for instance relationships, self-expression, and nature. People are putting their needs first and want to support/work/invest in organizations that help them to succeed and be happy. Today's workforce has seen too much and work is going to be taking a backseat to life. How do companies pivot to re-humanize the work experience and align with New Essentialism?

The real risk to your business over the next ten years is people. Think about that idea. People can turn against you quickly and at scale, and in a VUCA world anything is possible. If you do not have a strong positive relationship to weather any kind of storm, you are in a perilous place. You need committed people. Think of your people—from your lead investor to your frontline employees to every customer—as your volunteer force. They are here because they are passionately committed and truly want to be. For you, this is about re-imagining and redesigning the human side of your business. Building an Enchanted Brand is a big part of it.

PEOPLE ARE VULNERABLE

Although the Pandemic brought people to a new reckoning point where they freed themselves to better adapt and flourish in the new world, this did not diminish the effects of constant change. People are still in a vulnerable, fragile state. The world remains in flux, causing deep angst due to the severity of constant change – of which there is no end in sight. Unexpected and frequently shocking events that assault personal values and one's understanding of the world (and their place within it) continue - climate change events, random mass violence, fatal weather, revolutionizing technologies e.g. dark web, space travel, auto-driving cars. People are struggling with incongruity, confusion and uncertainty which evokes fears, frustrations and anger. Companies and organizations are at the center of it all as they are the mechanisms driving change. As people struggle to find answers and some control in a world they cannot understand, they keep it simple. They look for villains and saviors. Your company is one or the other.

People are increasingly aware of what is going on in the world (heavy media exposure) and questioning how and why things are happening. Who is responsible? They are desperately looking for solutions for a better way of life, better world, and organizations who can bring it. You can win be becoming a part of the solution and helping people to be part of the solution. Jump on that bandwagon and add a turbo charger. You'll find that it saves your organization in the worst of times and amplifies success in the best. It will bring the committed people you need at all levels.

Where do you begin? Building an Enchanted Brand is a starting point, because it is a relationship bridge built on an emotional connection. It is deeply human and personal, not transactional and anonymous. Think about building a brand that improves a person's life experience in a VUCA world. Think about how to strengthen personal resiliency, optimism and vision, so your brand empowers people to stay steady and advance in an unending stormy sea of change. By building an Enchanted Brand, you become part of the solution. No matter what kind of widget you make or sell, an Enchanted Brand will enable your organization to transcend barriers and challenges brought on by your greatest variable—people.

THE VUCA MINDSET

Based on what we've covered, there are some trends to keep in mind as you think about re-building the human side of your business. In general, people are more skeptical about institutions, fiercely withhold trust, and show reluctance to go above and beyond and to sacrifice their time, life, and family for company interests. Work and the employer no longer sit on the throne and call all the shots. People are calling their own shots and taking their own chances. Support that change in roles.

Everyone is on the lookout for truth and authenticity. They want to know what to believe in, and what to get behind. Facts alone don't provide the answer, because facts get diffused with scrutiny. You have to pair facts with context—ideas—in order for them to stick—be embraced and believed. In times of uncertainty, people rely more on their gut, instincts, and intuition. Get your facts and give them relevance with ideas that matter to your people.

I don't believe people are turning into cynics. On the contrary, I think people remain optimistic despite all the challenges, but that optimism is tinged with fear. This is a great opportunity for your organization—dispel the fear and feed the optimism. People desperately want a way forward. Your Enchanted Brand can help them find it and act on it.

Think about your investors. Your leadership team, employees, customers, vendors, partners, influencers, and the public. This is the human side of your business. How do build an experience that contributes to everyone's life? How do you bring them all together around a common campfire? How do you empower each personal journey? You can do all of the above by building an Enchanted Brand.

ENCHANTING YOUR BRAND

People are led by their hearts. Despite best efforts to be rational, we are emotional, intuitive beings. You must focus on forging a strong, authentic emotional connection where people understand that you are on their side and are making their lives and the world a better place instead of exploiting them for financial gain. We are talking love (some form of affinity) and loyalty. Without it, the wheels can come off the bus at the slightest curve in the road. Head it off at the pass. Reduce that risk. Build the connection.

The Enchanted Brand is a tool to build that relationship. Think of it is a piece of powerful art, created specifically to connect everyone around the same idea and ideals, and where your product or company is the enabler. The brand, in some regards, represents an epic narrative of positive possibilities. It opens minds, allows people to see things differently, and empowers them to take action and grow. With that kind of brand, you can do anything. But you have to create it first and then stand behind it. Treat it like the priceless asset it is. This why powerful brands are always governed by the CEO.

Brand power flows from the corner office. If the CEO believes in the brand, prioritizes the brand, speaks about the brand and protects it, everyone follows. On the contrary, if the CEO rarely speaks about the brand and doesn't have conviction, brand faith rings hollow. It is nearly impossible to build a powerful brand without a CEO as the champion. From Walt Disney to Andy Grove (Intel) to Steve Jobs (Apple) to Ralph Larsen (Johnson and Johnson) to Phil Knight (Nike), Ken Chenault (American Express) and beyond, you'll find legendary CEO's led with a powerful brand and made brand building a company-wide responsibility.

TAKEAWAYS

- People are the driver of your future, and they are more volatile and unpredictable than ever.
- There is no longer tolerance for maximizing shareholder value at all costs. People must come before profits.
- Work is no longer in the catbird seat as post-pandemic people relegate work to a lesser role, one that they can control.
- To hire great talent and achieve high performance, you will need to change requirements and put employee happiness first.
- The Enchanted Brand allows you to forge the trust, loyalty, and affinity needed to keep all people, from investors to frontline employees to customers and the general public, supporting your organization in a VUCA world.

QUESTIONS TO EXPLORE

- Where does your organization compromise or marginalize people for the good of the organization?
- What actions could be taken to put people first?
- What could you do to enable your employees and customers to live happier lives?
- What would need to change for the organization to embrace a "people first" directive?

5

Enchantment Is the Answer: Thriving in a VUCA World

"Want to change the world? Change caterpillars into butterflies? This takes more than run-of-the-mill relationships. You need to convince people to dream the same dream that you do. That's a big goal, but one that's possible for all of us"
— **Guy Kawasaki**[60]

THE IMAGINATION AND ENCHANTMENT

THINK OF THE IMAGINATION AS A MUSCLE, A MUSCLE NEEDED for heavy lifting in a VUCA world. Because the VUCA world presents us with unexpected and unthinkable realities on a continual basis, it requires us to absorb change and positively adapt if we are to grow. To do so with minimal friction, disruption, and stress requires a kind of resilience that comes from a healthy, active imagination. The more we can imagine, the more comfortable we become with newness, novelty, and unexpected possibilities. A strong imagination may very well be the defining human trait for success in a VUCA world.

The challenge is that imagination is a muscle that has largely been underused. How often do you use your imagination? Imagination is what will allow people to embrace the novel and the inconceivable and to see their way through the unknown and uncertain. Imagination is what will give credence to hope, because if people can't imagine it, they can't believe in it. Think of your investors, employees, customers, and all the people important to your organization. If they are not to be daunted, defeated, and dissuaded by the challenges of a VUCA world and if you want to mitigate the risks of their unpredictable behavior, strengthen their imaginations. Give them a greater ability to thrive in uncertainty and ambiguity. Many people don't know how to activate their imagination and are at a big disadvantage in the VUCA world. Enchantment stimulates the imagination, so it is a tool for strengthening people in a VUCA world.

"The imagination is cognitive peripheral vision that helps us 'see' all of those things that are lying just out of range of what we know. And helps us discover things unknown."
— Anne M. Pendleton-Jullian, interview
with Henry Jenkins, 2016[68]

Throughout history, enchantment has been used to help people accept the problematic nature of life without being defeated by it. During times of great human struggle, such as World Wars I and II, enchanting music, entertainment, and advertising filled the culture (see sidebar). People grabbed onto it to cope, hope, and work for a better future. Struggling against severe difficulties is unavoidable, particularly in our new world, and is an intrinsic part of human existence. In a VUCA world, however, struggle is relentless with no end in sight. Things seem to be fine and then *bam*, they are not. Extreme disruption. Here, we need enchantment to strengthen people to meet the unexpected and emerge victorious.

Bruno Bettelheim, legendary child psychologist, explored the power of enchantment in studying fairy tales. Bettelheim recognized the unconscious as a powerful determinant of behavior in a child or adult. He discovered that when unconscious material is permitted to come to awareness and is worked through in the imagination, its potential for causing harm is reduced; and the opportunity to produce positive contributions is increased. He found that fairy tales provide a unique way for children to come to terms with the dilemmas of their inner lives and a world that is often bewildering. Fairy tales helped to develop the capability to understand oneself in a complex world where a person must learn to cope and thrive. Sound familiar? This is like all of us in a VUCA world. Enchanted Brands will be our fairy tales. Explaining to a child why a fairy tale is so captivating destroys the enchantment. Part of the power of enchantment is that one is not quite sure why one is delighted. This is the magic.

According to Guy Kawasaki, from his work with Apple and across businesses, when done right, enchantment is more powerful than traditional persuasion, influence, or marketing techniques. It literally defies logic. It connects to our emotional and intuitive minds instead of our rational minds. It can turn decisions your way even when hard facts are against you. It can convert hostility into civility and civility into affinity, change skeptics into believers and the undecided into the loyal.[62] For anyone who has had the benefit of working with an enchanting brand, the testimonials will be the same. The brand carries the day against all odds. Remember the Tylenol crisis of 1982? It was the Johnson & Johnson brand that saved the day.[63]

Enchantment happens in the imagination and can be triggered at any time—during a retail transaction, a high-level corporate negotiation, on a social media post, and even on a package. When you put enchantment into your brand, you are able to bring it everywhere the brand travels and to benefit from its magic.

Think of enchantment has done for these brands:

• Turned a cooler company called Yeti into a outdoor lifestyle company worth more than $700 billion.

• Transformed a fiber optic construction company called Qwest into the fourth-largest telecom company after ATT, Sprint, and MCI.

• Catapulted a West Coast fashion company named DOEN into the impenetrable world of high fashion with one of the most passionate brand communities since Apple.

• Built Black Rifle Coffee into a new coffee empire.

Enchantment is noteworthy. In these days, we are more familiar with feelings of disenchantment, disillusionment and despair. I believe that our capacity to be enchanted is crucial to our mental, spiritual, and perhaps even our physical well-being. In a mechanistic and material existence, enchantment shines a light on how little we actually know; and, that knowing isn't everything.

Finding your way to enchantment is a thrilling endeavor. Your capacity to be enchanted has never been lost and we will explore how to open it in chapter 14. Enchantment has much to teach us about hidden wonders blocked by our over-analytical minds. Enchantment releases us into a world beyond thought in which perceptions and sensations lead the way to awe. Right now, let yourself muse on the possibility of enchantment.

HOW ENCHANTMENT WORKS

Enchantment is a little like love. It's hard to explain. It's delightful—a transcendent experience that puts you into a feel-good place. You fall into it seamlessly and it captures you effortlessly. You surrender to it unexpectedly. The Tiffany box, the Disney castle, and even the rugged, rough uncomfortable ride of a Harley Davidson bike are all enchanting brand experiences. Part of the power of enchantment is that one is not quite sure why one is delighted. And it all takes place in our imagination. That's the key. Enchantment stimulates and exercises the imagination—the very capability people need to thrive in a VUCA world. It helps people transcend to another place and see beyond what is before them.

The great social theorist Max Weber was a fan of enchantment. He believed the world was a "great enchanted garden" (as do I) and that life was full of mystery. In a 1917 lecture, he talked about "the disenchantment of the world" where he described a world where reason and science could explain all natural and human phenomena and resulted in depleted and shrunken universe.[65] If all things are knowable, explainable, and manipulable, and if we live in a universe governed by knowable natural laws and mastered by human will, life would be quite boring. I couldn't agree more. Let's not cover up the enchanted garden. Later, the German theologian and philosopher Rudolf Otto adopted the term "numinous," based on the Latin word *numen* (divine power) to describe enchantment as an experience of awe and surprise, "a non-rational, non-sensory experience or feeling whose primary and immediate object is outside the self."[66] Psychologist William James described it as "shaken free from the cage of self."[67] By definition, enchantment refers to being under a magic spell or charm, a feeling of great pleasure or delight. Brands are vehicles that can capture and share enchantment for the betterment of individual lives, communities, and humanity at large.

THE ENCHANTED BRAND

Looking back, we have enchanting brands in our history. Looking forward, we need a lot more and these new Enchanted Brands need to have a different structure, because we live in a different time.

Enchanted Brands are built on the foundation of traditional brands but are fundamentally different in their roles. They exist to serve people instead of selling products, and thereby create a meaningful human connection in a world where connections are fleeting and fragile. The new Unique Selling Proposition (USP) is embedded in the new essentialism and connects a company or product to it in an enchanting, conceptual way. Enchanted Brands are abstractions with authentic roots. They are deeply human, tethered to new human truths. They are idea-driven, delightful, and uplifting. They help people transcend the noise of reality to think, feel, and act in a personally authentic way. Acting as public art rather than advertising, they don't tell you how to think and feel—they liberate you to think and feel for yourself.

In the Enchanted Brand paradigm, brands would be less commercial and slick, but still retain a sense of ambition by becoming more relevant, permeable, and participatory—a force people tap into when they want to soothe, share, reach out, scratch an itch, or solve a problem. The success of companies is increasingly going to depend on supporting and amplifying the value of that connected, participatory feeling produced from the company's brand. The ability of Enchanted Brands to engage and ignite the imagination is the capacity that helps humanity grow.

Unlike traditional brands, Enchanted Brands are not designed to manipulate people but, instead, to liberate them. To some, this might seem counterintuitive. Aren't brands meant to shape and direct for the purpose of making a sale? Yes. But Enchanted Brands shape and direct in a less prescriptive way and for the purpose of opening possibilities which, ideally, may include a sale. In other words, people are more involved in the mental equation.

Using the power of enchantment, these brands transform situations and relationships by bringing about a voluntary, enduring, and delightful change in people. By enlisting the goals and desires of people, by being likable and trustworthy, they enchant. Enchanted Brands can open hearts and minds and empower new actions, like a fairy tale on steroids. Based on using a provocative idea or metaphor, these brands inspire and empower people to have greater agency in the world. Wow—not to just buy something, but to grow and dive into the world with confidence and optimism. We need Enchanted Brands in our metamorphosing world to dispel fear of the unknown and the outrageous, to empower acceptance of the novel and unexpected, and to inspire human beings to grow.

WHAT IS AN ENCHANTED BRAND?

For those eager to get down to the practical, let's define an Enchanted Brand in an actionable way. An Enchanted Brand possesses these six characteristics:

1. *Intention:* Have a clear, relevant point to make
2. *Engaging:* Entertain and arouse curiosity
3. *Enriching:* Stimulate the imagination and clarify emotions
4. *Authentic:* Tethered to a compelling truth
5. *Aligned:* Attuned to anxieties and aspirations, give full recognition to difficulties while suggesting solutions
6. *Enabling:* Promote self-confidence and personal value and give agency—ability to have an impact on the world

An Arsenal for New Vulnerability

In periods of unrest (post-Depression, post-World War II, post-civil and economic strife of 1970s) when there was a search for new coherence, people turned to enchanted entertainment and brands to help them cope and move on. Procter & Gamble invented the soap opera after the Depression and Kellogg's cereal brands flourished by delivering enchantment with the slogan, "snap, crackle, and pop." During World War II, brands such as Dixie Cups and Birds Eye foods stressed patriotism. Other brands leveraged other ad themes—"the world of tomorrow," "Lucky Strike Means Fine Tobacco (L.S.M.F.T.)" powered the dancing Lucky Strike cigarettes, while such brands as Pan American Airways, Firestone Tire, and Esso came to life. In the 1940s, we saw the birth of Jeep and Estée Lauder. In the mid-1970s, McDonald's became enchanting. When people were feeling unmoored, daunted, in transition, uncertain, and even overwhelmed, enchantment gave them inner strength and optimism to move on.

As companies face a new vulnerability—people—they need a new arsenal. The Enchanted Brand, once built, can be leveraged to help meet the new demands of, and challenges with, investors, employees, partners and vendors, consumers, competitors, analysts, and the general public.

Now, let's dive into how you can build an Enchanted Brand.

TAKEAWAYS

- The imagination is a muscle that needs to be strong to succeed in a VUCA world.
- Enchantment strengthens the imagination.
- Brands can capture and distribute enchantment.
- Unlike traditional brands, Enchanted Brands serve rather than sell and stimulate the imagination.
- Enchanted Brands are vehicles for improving the human side of business.

QUESTIONS TO EXPLORE

- Think about an enchanting brand experience. What did you find enchanting about it? Write it down.
- Think of three brands that you find enchanting. Write down what is enchanting about them.
- At this moment, if there is one thing that might be enchanting about your brand, write it down.

6

Brand Basics: What Is a Brand and How Does It Work?

O N THE JOURNEY TO BUILDING AN ENCHANTED BRAND, IT'S important for you to understand what a brand actually is and how it works. This chapter will clear away any confusing cobwebs that may be clouding up your mind and give you the mental mastery needed to build an Enchanted Brand.

WHAT IS A BRAND?

"A man hears what he wants to hear and disregards the rest." —**Paul Simon, "The Boxer"**[75]

Ultimately, the brand is a mental construct that resides in the mind and influences interpretation and behavior. Although trademarked by a company that owns it, a brand is a set of associations that come to life in the imagination of people. I give you a diamond ring in a Tiffany box and I give you the same diamond ring in a Walmart box. Is there a difference for you? There is if you know the brands. The brand shapes how you interpret the value of what it represents. Before going further, let's dive deeper into the basic understanding of a brand.

Brand	Poland Springs Fiji	Coke Pepsi	Yeti Igloo	Visa American Express Venmo

Although often confused with the products, services, and companies they represent, brands are a separate thing. A brand is not a logo. It is not a product. It is not a company. It's not the packaging, advertising, or tagline. Although people use the term "brand" and "branding" to mean multiple things, which causes confusion, the brand is actually a set of mental associations that exist in the mind. For powerful brands, these associations have been deliberately created. They have not occurred by accident. They are the result of a well-designed brand identity, or creative concept, being consistently expressed over time in lots of ways—for example, in the logo, product packaging, and advertising tagline.

Brands are often confused with the products the represent, but...

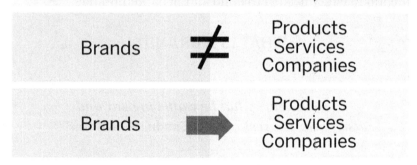

Yes, brands are a repository of associations, beliefs, and feelings that exist in the mind, and which are consistently activated by seeing a signifier of the brand—name, logo, packaging, product, and maybe even a smell (think Play-Doh). For powerful brands, these associations are linked by a single idea; for instance, Campbell's Soup is anchored by the idea of mother's love. The brand is a rich conceptual framework with various threads that weave together to produce desire by evoking thoughts and feelings. Think of the brand as a piece of art and think about how art works. The artist is speaking to you in largely symbolic terms, yet you get the message.

Apple
Unleash The Power Of Your Creativity
(With Radically Easy-To-Use Technology)

Nike
Pursue Your Passion
(Empowered By Superior Athletic Products)

Another way to think about your brand is that it is a lens in the mind through which people interpret reality. This lens helps us to rapidly sort, organize, and process information—and prioritize it. Is this important to me? How do I feel about this? If the lens is "a greedy pharmaceutical company," I will see the actions and products through that lens. If the lens is a loving healthcare company, I will interpret the same actions and products differently.

The Brand is a Mental Lens That Acts As a Filter to Interpret Reality

REALITY	BRAND LENS	PERCEPTIONS
Actions		Relevance, Value
Products		Trust
Culture		Affinity
What Others Say		Reputation
Events		Associations

Think about how you view the same exact product with a different brand lens. What associations come to your mind?

Brands do not live in the tangible world. Their world is the mind. Products go on shelves; brands live in the brain. Products come and go; brands endure in the memory. Can you think of brands that exist in your mind where the company or product exist no more? Woolworth? Pan Am? Prodigy? Products and marketing can be copied—and often are—but brands are as unique as fingerprints. Rarely does a brand try to copy and encroach on another brand. The best example is when rival Unilever launched Surf as a replicate brand of Procter & Gamble's longstanding detergent leader Tide and rapidly grew to category leadership.

- Similar name: Tide and Surf
- Similar packaging: related imagery
- Similar advertising: better living through cleaner clothes
- Same price point

BRANDS ARE GREATER THAN THE PRODUCTS THEY REPRESENT

A successful brand establishes the ideal lens in the mind and influences behavior accordingly. This brand, however, is not a factual lens, although every brand needs credibility. It is a fictional lens with authentic roots. For example, for decades the Volvo brand stood for safety, although there are safer cars on the market from brands such as Mercedes Benz. What makes Jeep uniquely qualified to own adventure when there are other, more rugged vehicles out there? Unlike a product promise, a brand promise is conceptual and aspirational, not literal.

POWERFUL BRANDS ARE BASED ON BIG IDEAS

Brands are concepts, not messages. The bigger the concept, the bigger the power. Consider Acura and BMW. When Acura launched as Honda's luxury automotive brand, it focused on "precision-crafted performance." I'd argue that's more of a message than an idea. We all know the BMW brand stands for the ultimate driving machine enabled by German engineering excellence. A big idea supported by a true, original concept. BMW has a mind-expanding notion—taking consumers to a place of imagining their dream cars—and evokes an emotional response.

Powerful Brands Are Built Upon "Mind Expanding" Notions That Get People To See The World Differently

Discovery and Adventure

"Join the Navy and see the world"

Enhancing Life

"Things go better with Coke"

Personal Connection

"Reach Out and Touch Someone with AT&T"

Brands own big ideas and these big ideas, because they grab people in their tenders, are able to transcend reality. They usher in a framework that transforms value. Historically, Avis was a struggling loser brand with second-rate customer service, living in the shadows of dominant Hertz, until it became a hardworking underdog with the branding idea, "we try harder." People connected to it, gave Avis another shot, forgave its inability to deliver adequate service (it's trying) and the business grew to become a viable rival to Hertz. The classic Harley Davidson brand—American rugged individualism—elevated a product that was heavy, loud, and hard to handle into a longstanding category leader. Marlboro, leveraging the American cowboy mythology, continues to sell a product that can kill you and remains the best-selling cigarette brand in the world. Against all reason (we are not rational beings), powerful brands help businesses and products transcend reality.

When JetBlue first took to the air in 2000, it was launched as a discount airline, but in doing so it also cleverly created a premium brand focused on bringing humanity and enjoyment to air travel. Aside from low fares, the JetBlue brand helped people appreciate things, because it was the first airline to offer live TV. Before long, JetBlue was winning numerous awards and was being touted as the best domestic airline—not just the best discount airline. It soon established a market value that nearly matched that of United, American, and Delta combined and became recognized as a premium brand.

BRANDS CAN DETRACT VALUE

It's not all rosy with brands. Sometimes a brand is in the mind, and it is full of misperceptions or obsolete truths that affect a business. Sometimes even one misperception can alter a company's reality. Hence the amount of rebranding work that is done to update that filter.

Before Samsung rebranded in early 2000, the brand actually took away value from the product. When I was working with Samsung during that time, they were convinced that bringing their products to the U.S. market under the Samsung name at a price significantly below the market leader Sony would be a slam dunk. After all, Sony was taking Samsung products and putting their brand on them and achieving market leadership. Basically, Samsung was an original equipment manufacturer to Sony. The plan to bring the exact same consumer electronic products to market under the Samsung name failed to account for the brand. What happened? Sales were very low and product returns were high. When investigating the problem, we discovered a brand issue. When people saw the Samsung brand, the only thing they knew was that it was Korean. The big idea was—Korean. Given inaccurate common knowledge about Korea, outdated associations with the country and encounters with cheap Korean made products, the Samsung brand suffered. Samsung meant "cheap, copycat products from a third-world manufacturer trying to look like Sony." Korea, of course, is not a third-world country, but brands are more often about fiction, not fact. This misconception compelled the company to build the brand we know today. While Sony products flew off the shelf, Samsung products initially did not, and customer dissatisfaction was exponentially higher with Samsung than for Sony branded products (even though the product was the same). Samsung retrenched and rebuilt its brand. In 2020, Samsung ranked number five on Interbrand's list of the best global brands.[69]

Historical Brand Example: Consumer Electronics

REALITY	SONY BRAND LENS	PERCEPTIONS	OUTCOMES
Same Consumer Electronics Products Sold Under Two Different Brands		Japanese Superior Quality Well-Made Innovative	High Sales Premium Price Low Returns
	SAMSUNG BRAND LENS		
		Korean-made Cheap Quality Copycat Questionable Performance Unreliable	Slow Sales Low price High Returns

Staying relevant is the biggest challenge in a rapidly changing world. Brand value can shift quickly, because brands are context sensitive. Their value is based on needs, wants, and dreams. If those change, the brand can find itself out of tune.

AN OCEAN OF CHOICE
AND SEAS OF SAMENESS

Nowadays, virtually everything is "branded" or least named. Nielsen Media Research lists more than 500,000 brands worldwide in more than 2,000 product categories.[70] Just ten year ago, no one could have imagined a world with this many products, brands and messages.

- There are over 20 million e-commerce sites in 2020.[71]
- Roughly 399,000 U.S. patents were issued in 2020, compared to only 66,000 in 1980.[72]
- The average American sees 6,000 to 10,000 advertising messages a day compared to 5,000 a day in 2007.[73]

Remember, you may be operating in a small industry, but the people you are targeting—customers, investors, employees—live in a crowded, confusing world of products and brands where there is very little differentiation and lots of blurring. What makes it worse is that many named products are not brands. They are just products with names and clever marketing. This only adds to the numbing effect of sameness we all know all too well. Many are grabbing the same overripe fruit, and as a result brands are beginning to look the same. I call this the "blanding" problem.

Brands exist to differentiate, yet surprisingly many do not. We live in an age of brand parity, a true oxymoron. Brands today mostly just blur together in our minds. Very few have the budgets (Apple, Geico, and others spend $1 billion or more a year on advertising[74]) or bold ideas that allow them to do what brands are supposed to do. When branding is completely relegated to the marketing group, which is often entrenched in the status quo and protecting its value, I find companies play it safe and operate at the lowest level of branding. Thus, most contribute to a sea of indistinguishable brands.

Others follow obsolete rules of branding, such as believing a brand is all about attributes or simply communicating unique product features and functionality in a cool way. This is where advertising and branding differ. Great advertising might be about selling product differences in relevant and creative ways, but great branding is about owning an idea that links to those differences. Most brands don't live up to their potential because either their marketing department is using advertising practices or allowing the advertising agency to drive the branding.

Let me clarify the difference between creative product messaging versus a brand idea. For example, if you want people to believe a product is innovative, great-tasting, or the best, just saying so does not make it so, no matter how many times you say it or how creatively you say it. When you use a brand idea to evoke those beliefs in someone's mind, then you've convinced them because they made the decision. You use the brand as a stimulus to create a response in someone's mind. That is branding. Messages often dictate. Brands, like art, allow people to make their own conclusions. When companies only communicate messages, rather than build a brand, they create benign brands that add little value.

BRAND HISTORY IN A NUTSHELL

Brands have been around since ancient times. The well-known cattle branding crossed the Atlantic from Spain. "Trademarks" were used long before that by potters and silversmiths to identify their products.[76] Decorative signs hung on inns and taverns served the same purpose. Legally, a brand is a trademark. During the second half of the nineteenth century, branding evolved into an advanced marketing tool. The Industrial Revolution created a wealth of products that needed differentiation to compete and elevate value above commodity status. New communication systems made it easier and more necessary for companies to advertise. As manufacturers gained access to national markets, numerous brand names were born that would achieve legendary U.S. and global status.

After arriving on the scene largely after the Civil War, brands have gained importance during recent history as purchasers have been given myriad product choices. In an era of relative product scarcity, the product itself defined a person. For example, once just owning a car—any car—made you somebody in society. Brand did not matter. With the explosion of lots of cars from different manufacturers, all of which got you from point A to point B with many similar functions and features, brands became a way to differentiate. Do you own a Prius? Do you drive a Jeep? Or are you a Porsche person? With the explosion of manufactured goods and consumer choice, companies and consumers came to rely on brands to add another layer of differentiated meaning and value. The brand not only helped with the purchase decision, it gave meaning to consumption. It said something about the person, because they made the brand choice.

The nineteenth-century German sociologist Max Weber discovered that people recognize and identify with members of their own social class through shared means of consumption. In other words, the products we buy are bursting with symbolic meaning, and what people consume says something about who they are. In an age of relative product scarcity, people could tell the world who they were by conspicuously consuming more and better-quality goods than anyone else. For example, growing up in the 1920s, owning a car—any car—meant that you were somebody. And in the 1950s, owning your first color television set or air conditioner meant that you had achieved middle-class status.

With the explosion of manufactured goods, however, all of that changed. As a greater volume of products became available for less money, simply owning a product lost its symbolic value for consumers.

How Brands Historically Created Value

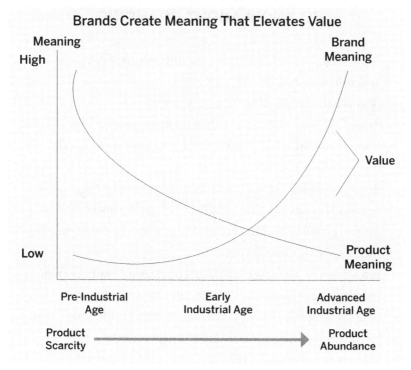

The law of supply and demand tells us that as supply increases to satisfy demand, profit margins and revenues created by the sale of products should decline. Interestingly, however, this did not happen. Instead, a new way to create value emerged—brands. Through brands, products and services were imbued with more meaning than they had ever possessed before. Brands introduced a new level of distinction through concept. In turn, these new distinctions led to a new economic paradigm that reinvigorated profit margins.

Today, it's the kind of car, the kind of television set, and the kind of sneakers you wear that communicates who you are. Brands have become the story icons of modern times.

TWELVE THINGS EVERY CEO NEEDS TO KNOW ABOUT BRANDING

- A powerful brand will dramatically improve performance and mitigate risk.
- Brand can create value in many ways.
- Branding does not equal advertising or marketing.
- Everything speaks for the brand, and everyone speaks for the brand.
- Brands are not logos, products, companies or taglines, but powerful concepts that reside in people's minds.
- Although trademarked by us, brands are living memories that reside in the culture.
- Brands form an interpretative lens that colors how people see and experience things; we can shape that lens.
- Brands simplify decisions, which is why people use them.
- Brands have the power to defy logic.
- In a world of brand parity, brands need an extreme difference of value.
- In a world of brand warfare, branding must be central to the business model.
- Brands are highly context-sensitive and must continually evolve over time.
-

TAKEAWAYS

- The word "brand" means different things at different times. It is both a means and an end.
- A brand is not a product, name, package, logo, or tagline. Ultimately, is a repository of beliefs and associations that reside in the memory.
- A brand is a lens in the mind that shapes interpretation and influences behavior.
- Most brands are on low power and contribute to a sea of sameness.
- Branding and advertising are often confused, but they are not the same.

QUESTIONS TO EXPLORE

- When people hear or see your brand, what comes to their mind and why? Which associations are valuable, and which are not?
- Do you have a brand strategy driving your brand value or is your brand the outcome of marketing activities and or the outside world?

7

Brand Basics—Your Brand Can Be A Priceless Asset

WHILE MANY SEE BRANDING AS A FORM OF MARKETING, I've always seen it as a core business strategy. I am writing this book about branding driven by the goal of guiding readers safely past that loaded word to an understanding of the enormous business value a brand brings in a changing world. Although countless books and gurus have preached about branding, few sermons have pierced the corporate wing, where traditional thinking and old-fashioned ideas about branding prevail and keep branding underused. Many senior executives belittle branding largely because they don't understand it.

FOUNDERS AND LEADERS OFTEN UNDERVALUE BRAND

"Branding is something you do to cows. Branding is what you do when there's nothing original about your product. But there is something original about our products. Or at least there used to be."[77]

Those were the words of Roy Disney, nephew of Walt Disney, during his well-publicized argument with Michael Eisner over the future of Disney in 2004. While it may be surprising that even someone at the top of one of the world's most coveted brands could so fundamentally misunderstand branding, misconceptions like these abound in most companies today, regardless of their size or influence.

Most C-suite executives and board leaders have financial or operational backgrounds. Few have had any experience working with powerful brands. Branding is not an area they understand or trust, because they lack direct experience with it and it's not analytical. Most view branding as a marketing expense rather than a business strategy and are happy to relegate primary responsibility to marketing executives. I have yet to be in a board meeting where anyone is advocating for investing more money in the brand. It's even difficult to engage leadership in conversation about branding as it's not a priority for them. Of course, for CEOs like Steve Jobs (Apple), Bill Gates (Microsoft), Ralph Larsen (Johnson & Johnson), Ken Chenault (American Express) and others who work or worked with powerful brands, the brand is paramount.

Most executives confuse branding with marketing. They view it as a large expense with questionable return. While they may know the cost of maintaining a brand, they cannot measure the value of it in the same terms, which makes them uncomfortable. This inability to measure concrete value pushes branding down the value chain.

Branding is a form of soft power. Soft power has been defined as the ability to attract and co-opt, rather than coerce (contrast hard power). It involves shaping the preferences of others through appeal and attraction. Joseph Nye introduced the concept of "soft power" in the late 1980s and later defined it as "the ability to influence the behavior of others to get the outcomes one wants."[78] There are several ways one can achieve this: you can coerce them with threats; you can induce them with payments; or you can attract and co-opt them to want what you want. Although it's difficult to measure its effects, soft power helps win. There's not a political or military leader who doesn't want it. Every business leader should want it, too.

BRANDING AS BUSINESS STRATEGY

"Corporate strategy and brand strategy have to be aligned. You would say that was obvious, but we have so many clients where the brand department and marketing department are not even brought into the discussion of what the corporate strategy is, or are told it is confidential, and yet are expected to manage the brand."
—David Haigh, CEO, The Brand Finance Institute[79]

On a basic level, brands enable people to recognize the makers of goods or providers of services rapidly. Over time, brands build perceptions of quality, value, price-level, reliability, and many other traits that help buyers choose among market offerings. They are quick and highly abbreviated tools of communication that deliver value in an information-overloaded world. Although this is true, it is a shallow and blunt explanation of brands and their value. Brands are much more than that. Although implemented in marketing, along with other parts of the company, branding is soft power that is a part of fundamental business strategy and belongs with the CEO and leadership team.

Brands are critically important to a company's success in today's VUCA world. As disruptions proliferate, product life cycles shrink, marketplace boundaries disappear, and consumption declines, branding delivers a "soft power" sustainable advantage in the minds of the purchasing public, employees, investors, partners, and even competitors. By connecting a company, product, or service to a compelling idea that resonates emotionally, brands create unique desire that can stand strong against opposing forces. Whether they want to enter a market, open a market, widen leadership, increase prices, raise from the dead, scale, or protect against downside possibilities, a brand helps make it happen.

BUSINESS VALUE FROM BRANDS

Foremost, brands affect how people perceive your company, product, or service. The brand instantly answers questions. What are you? Why should I care? Why are you valuable to me? When they do this in a way that makes a unique emotional connection and forges trust, they begin operating on your behalf in a psychological dimension and deliver real results. Brands have proven to:

- *Accelerate adoption of a new products:* Animated movies released by Disney capture far greater box office returns.
- *Command a premium price:* Price and brand have a complex relationship. Branded goods are always more expensive than "store" or "generic" brands. Some "brand equity" is so high that it can command a significant premium, for instance Tiffany in jewelry. In some cases, high price may signal to others the consumer's wealth or social status. People pay more for products with powerful brands. Starbuck's coffee. Heineken beer. Federal Express delivery. Hertz rental car. Intel chips. Lego toys.
- *Protect companies under attack.* Marlboro continued to experience record growth even after its cigarettes were linked to user deaths, and the government mandated a warning label on its packaging.
- *Convey superiority with an inferior product.* Kodak's film product was inferior to Fujifilm, yet the brand held a dominant share. Ivory soap was so harsh it created dry hands, but the gentle, pure, Ivory brand kept it number one.

- *Overcome product failures:* Apple's bug-ridden Newton personal digital assistant did not sink the franchise. Nor did Coors Rocky Mountain Sparkling Water, Google Glass, or Burger King Satisfries derail loyal brand fans.
- *Commercialize products.* Who invented diet cola? Caffeine-free cola? Diet cherry cola? RC Cola did. It was the first cola company, but it had a weak brand. Power brands Coca-Cola and Pepsi scaled the innovations and built global empires.
- *Recruit and retain top talent.* Big brands attract high performers and build resumes. Just ask the folks at Disney, Apple, Patagonia, Deloitte, American Express, and BMW.
- *Inspire employees to perform.* Big brands attract high performers and build resumes. Just ask the folks at Disney, Apple, Patagonia, Deloitte, American Express, and BMW.
- *Rebound from disaster:* When seven people died from ingesting extra-strength Tylenol capsules criminally laced with cyanide in 1982, then-CEO James E. Burke credited the trustworthy reputation of the brand for saving the day. Within a year, Tylenol recaptured most business and suffered no longstanding downsides even though the company was accountable for the lethal mistake. Now contrast that with the longstanding negative legacy of the Exxon Valdez spill, where there were no fatalities.
- *Outperform on Wall Street:* Companies with powerful brands outperform top companies listed on the S&P 500 and Fortune 500 across revenue and profit.[80]
- *Attract investors:* Iconic investor Warren Buffet looks for two traits in a good investment—a low-cost manufacturer or a powerful brand. One reason is that power brands are seen as protective moats. Starbucks, Nike, Disney, and McDonald's all have wide economic moats largely due to their brand power.[81]

Now that you understand the business value a brand can deliver, aside from the obvious differentiation and distillation of a complex value proposition, let's look into how brands work. I like to boil this down to three brand superpowers: ability to be noticed and remembered; ability to shape perception and define meaning; and ability to create desire.

BRANDS COMMAND ATTENTION SO YOU STAND OUT AND ARE REMEMBERED

Think of brands as powerful pieces of cultural art. Given the unique power of art to attract attention and pierce indifference, brands are able to break through our culture's fog of information overload to create interest, attachment, and preference. If you consider products as black-and-white, then brands bring them into full color.

Also, like great art, brands are memorable and engaging, and they deliver an emotional advantage. They are not easily forgotten and often remembered with strong emotions. Brands work because despite our best efforts at being rational, people are emotional, intuitive beings.

BRANDS SET CONTEXT THAT GIVES MEANING AND VALUE

The value of your company, product, or service may be obvious to you, but not to your future customers or to the world. A product doesn't speak for itself. A brand speaks for it.

To set product value, a brand captures it in a way that matters to your current and future customers. The brand exists to delight them, not you. Brands are creative concepts that frame perceptions of reality which give things meaning. A brand makes a beer into a

Miller, a cheap store into a Walmart (rather than a Kmart), and a commodity tire into a Michelin. Snickers became the number one candy bar when the brand positioned the product as a mid-day snack that gave energy. Gatorade, a sugary drink line, hit its stride when it became a sports beverage and, later, a performance beverage. Soap, under the brand Dove, became part of natural women's beauty and then good women's health. The product remains the same and the brand sets the value.

Think of the anti-lock braking system, a revolutionary product at the time. When introduced by Volvo, this product represented a breakthrough in safety. When introduced by BMW, it became a breakthrough in performance. Which is it? Both. It depends on the brand view. When Procter & Gamble had an exciting innovation in soap, it would evaluate which soap or detergent brand would best bring that innovation to market. The product's value would be determined by the brand.

Brands Give Product Attributes Meaning

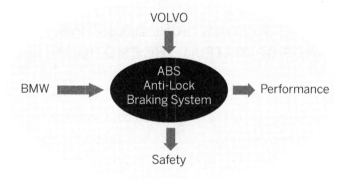

BRANDS CONNECT EMOTIONALLY

I used to wonder, what does that mean? Doesn't everything connect emotionally? What it means is that brands operate outside of rational analytics. They aren't convincing you with facts. Brands ignite preference and desire. They operate on the emotional part of the brain. Said another way, brands introduce the variable of love into the equation, and we all know the havoc that love can create. It's hard to fight against the tide of desire, no matter how many facts are on your side. How do brands create this desire? Many different ways. They often represent a valuable identity or desired aspiration. This preppy brand means you are a well-heeled person who is part of this American social class. Having clean clothes provided by this detergent is the sign of a good home. If your money is managed by this bank, you are smart and successful. If you drive this car, you are sexy or you love the environment or you are an adventurer—and so on. This also works for business goods sold to business buyers. We are all people.

EMOTIONS DRIVE DECISIONS, BRANDS OPERATE AT THE EMOTIONAL LEVEL

Emotions are the primary influencer in decision-making and emotions move faster than logic. They are central to risk evaluation, and risk evaluation is Darwinian because it's central to human survival. What makes a brand most valuable is that is persuades emotionally. It operates on another level from everything else a company does.

Essence of Brand Power

Emotional Processing		Rational Processing

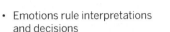

Emotional Processing	Rational Processing
• Emotions rule interpretations and decisions	• Logic rules interpretation and decision
• Information processing is automatic and effortless	• Information processing requires a deliberate effort to think it through
• Can pre-screen before we are consciously aware of it (like when you are startled by something before you know what it is)	• Logical and deductive approach to analyzing what appears
• Handles vast amounts of information quickly and simultaneously	• Limitations on what can be absorbed
• Rapid parallel procession	• Slow, linear, serial processing

Something can be valid, if you want it to be	For something to be valid, it requires empirical evidence and logical argument

Emotions act as the primary influencer in making any kind of decision. Even in apparently conscious decision-making, emotions are always at play, whether you're deciding what car to buy, what stock to invest in, or what to eat for dinner, it doesn't matter how much data you collect and how many consultants you bring in to help you reach a decision. A study conducted by neuroscientist Antonio Damasio found that people who suffered from damage to the part of the brain where emotions are generated had an impaired ability to make decisions.[82] They could logically describe what they should be doing, but in practice found it difficult to make basic decisions about such things as where to live and what to eat.

When a snake jumps out at you, without thinking you automatically jump back before you realize that the snake is caged and can't hurt you. The situation happens so quickly that there's no time to become aware of how you should consciously feel. Your emotions, which process quickly, drive the behavior.

The Five Sins of Brand Vanity

Does your company suffer from brand vanity? Below are the five common sins of brand vanity that prevent companies from building a powerful brand.

Research shows our brand is doing well. Research shows the brand is loved, admired, and trusted. That may mean something, but it depends on its relative value. How do the scores compare relative to your competition? You can't just examine your brand in a vacuum. Is the brand possibly at a plateau? Examining the brand in a vacuum is a vanity point that may cause the brand to become tarnished, lose its edge, and become obsolete over time.

The brand is creating value. The brand may be creating value, but is it the right value? Maybe the brand is evoking associations, beliefs, and images that helped your company in the past, but are not that helpful now. Brands need to be stewarded so they can evolve. The question is not, "Is the brand strong?" but, "Is the brand strong enough to help us move into the future?" Past performance is not the best indicator of future success on Wall Street or Main Street. Know what you need your brand to do and evolve it to do so.

We have a great advertising campaign. People often confuse brands with advertising. If people love the advertising campaign, they may or may not love the brand. Be sure to evaluate the brand, not just the advertising. Great advertising is valuable, but it needs to build lasting brand equity; otherwise, the value is fleeting.

This brand is an institution. When your brand is an icon or an institution, people are afraid to touch it. Yet, market conditions change quickly, and a company can get caught behind the eight-ball if it doesn't use its brand to lead the way. This is how brands atrophy. Think about brands that once commanded great cultural influence, and now are just well-known names. Dell, Hewlett-Packard, Harley-Davidson, MTV, Avon, and America Online are some examples. Keep the brand on a path of continual improvement by sharpening the edges, and by asking the question, "What is working, what is not, and what makes this brand powerful today and in the future?"

We have a strong corporate reputation. Your company may have a corporate reputation without a strong brand. For example, IBM has a strong corporate reputation, but there is nothing magical about the brand. In fact, I'm hard pressed to know what the branding idea is that connects IBM to its audience? Reputations are built from reliable quality, service, and integrity. Often, they rely on history, and that reliance makes them vulnerable. A brand narrative contributes to the reputation but is not the same thing. The brand narrative operates apart from the reputation and provides conceptual and emotional equity.

William James, the grandfather of modern psychology, was among the first to reject the theory that our brain tells our body how to react to a situation. Instead, he posited that that emotions flow from the body to the brain. The brain surveys the body, notices the skin sweating or the heart beating quickly, and then infers the emotion that matches the physical signals that the body has generated.

It's not all about emotions, but a combination of emotions and logic. Some of us learned this idea from *Star Trek*. Yes, sometimes Gene Roddenberry's *Star Trek* television series of the 1960s has the answers to it all. Dr. Spock was the Vulcan who adhered to logic—although he did have a human heart—and was the counterbalance to Dr. McCoy, who was all emotion. If you just go down Spock's track, you lose. If you just go down Dr. McCoy's track, you lose. You need a brand with logical attributes and an emotional connection—and vision. Yes, Captain James Tiberius Kirk. Kirk is the brand that integrates both Spock's and McCoy's perspectives with vision and ingenuity.

A classic real-world example can be found in the "diapers war" between Pampers and Huggies in the late 1970s. Before Huggies entered the market, Procter & Gamble dominated disposable diapers with a purely rational value proposition—superior absorbency. Pampers were the most absorbent diapers in the world, and the ad campaigns showed how quickly Pampers diapers absorbed liquids. In the late 1970s, Kimberly-Clark introduced Huggies and changed the game. Rather than basing its brand on a rational claim to a higher-quality product, it centered the Huggies brand on a simple emotional desire: happy babies. What parent of a newborn doesn't want a happy baby? The brand had an immediate, emotional trigger based on an enduring universal truth—the fact that adoring parents will do almost anything to ensure the happiness of their babies. With this proposition, Huggies eroded

Pampers' market share, eventually capturing leadership of the U.S. diaper market. Huggies has been the highest-selling diaper in America since 1993 and is now the number one or number two brand in over eighty countries.

Now you understand the unique powers of the brand asset in your arsenal. Companies that are not proactively building powerful brands are not pursuing value and growth with full force. Even brilliant innovators need a powerful brand. Where would Apple be without its brand? Or Nike? Or Johnson & Johnson? Brands add value even when growth is delivered by innovation or a rock star CEO. Anyone can do it, but it requires courage, an investment in the consumer relationship and using practices that work.

Today We Live In An Age of "Brand" Marketing

We are no longer simply selling products/services ➡️ We are now selling a **brand**

Microsoft

⬇️

Expressed in products/services

TAKEAWAYS

- Most senior executives misunderstand and undervalue branding.
- Branding is fundamental business strategy, not a marketing strategy.
- Brands have proven to defy logic and deliver business value in multiple ways.
- Decisions are emotionally driven, and brands operate at the emotional level.
- Brands combine vision, logic, and emotion to connect and persuade.

QUESTIONS TO EXPLORE

- On a scale of one to ten, how invested is your leadership team in branding?
- What is the biggest obstacle to embracing branding as a valuable asset?
- If you could change one thing about your brand to make it more powerful for driving your business forward, what would it be?

8

Building an Enchanted Brand

WE'VE COVERED WHAT ENCHANTMENT IS AND HOW IT works. We've explored the basics of branding and what it takes to create a powerful brand. Now, let's bring these two together and jump into branding to the next level of branding by creating an Enchanted Brand.

WHY ARE ENCHANTED BRANDS SO IMPORTANT?

Foremost, because traditional brands are disappearing into a marketing sales funnel just when businesses and people need the conceptual and emotional power of brands more than ever. On the business side, people are becoming increasingly volatile and distrustful of institutions, facts, and authority. Their behavior is increasingly unpredictable and, with modern tools, can be quite powerful. On the human side, our metamorphosizing world, with its onslaught of controlling technologies, may be robbing humanity of its essence. In this complex world where systems create unthinkable events, often without notice, human beings are experiencing something never faced before—and it is unrelenting. It is truly a new world with new rules. Chances are, we have no idea what this world is really doing to any of us. Enchanted Brands offer a way to help preserve our humanity—what we value most—and a way to strengthen people so they adapt and grow in a VUCA world rather than become defeated and subsumed by it. It may sound lofty, but do not underestimate the important cultural role brands play. Like great art and music, they can shape minds and move people to action.

Enchanted Brands are in public service. A fundamental difference between Enchanted Brands and traditional brands is that Enchanted Brands deliver social good by design. Although created by companies to deliver business value, they are built in a mindful way to serve humanity. They are cultural artifacts that preserve and nurture people by acting as a trigger of cultural memory. Enchanted Brands stimulate the imagination. As such, they can operate as a platform for sharing and debate, co-creation, and unity, and can cross borders and barriers to bridge differences. Enchanted Brands will keep us moored and feeling our humanity in a swirling world where everything seems upside down. They will remind us and inspire us. In this regard, Enchanted Brands are a powerful expression of corporate social responsibility, as companies need to be accountable for what their brands put into the culture. Imagine what might happen if just some of the hundreds of billions of dollars spent annually on traditional brands that sell, were spent on Enchanted Brands that serve? If we put those dollars to work in building Enchanted Brands that strengthen people, people will grow and reciprocate with brand preference, loyalty, and maybe even brand advocacy. It's a win, win, win.

We acknowledge that Enchanted Brands sell through service, not through exploiting unfulfilled dreams, unattainable aspirations, or identity crises. Like traditional powerful brands, Enchanted Brands are idea-based, but the ideas here are to awaken and enlarge the imagination—the superpower unique to humanity. These brands take off in the direction of delight, fantasy, challenge, inspiration, empathy, wonder, and awe, and they ignite "out of rational mind" thinking. Their Emotional Quotient (EQ) is much higher than traditional brands, because they operate on the enchanted plane where the mysterious relationship between dream and reality, the conscious and the unconscious minds, connect. Only by escaping the confines of the rational, can these brands pierce the well-guarded consciousness of the individual to work their magic.

WE START WITH THE HOLY TRINITY

Before we dive into what to do, let's establish a basic structure. This approach recognizes a distinction between three interrelated, and often confused, elements: reputation, brand, and corporate or product identity. Sometimes people conflate these to the detriment of all three. To build an Enchanted Brand, we acknowledge the unique role and value of each, and understand how they inform one another. Before engaging in a brand strategy, we need to understand this holy trio, which is intertwined, and must never be confused. The reputation is a series of perceptions related to the quality and values of the company and products. Corporate identity is a company-centric narrative that is strategic, largely spelling out who we are, what we do, and the unique value we bring. It features market positioning, the value proposition, strategic assets and core competencies, and competitive advantage. The brand builds on the corporate identity. The corporate identity is strategic and defines the story the company wants to tell. The brand is conceptual and defines the story the consumer wants to hear. Using consumer insight and tethered to the strategic imperatives of the corporate identity, the brand strives to embed meaning into the life of the consumer. It makes a promise that the consumer wants. The promise is backed by reasons a consumer can believe. The brand is built around a compelling idea that lights up the imagination of the consumer (opening their mind) and brings a humanizing personality. This is why brands connect with people and build an emotional bridge between companies and people.

Reputation: Much has been written about what a reputation is and how it works. For our purposes, know that there are beliefs and opinions held about your company and product that are often related to quality and trust, and sometimes focused on particular characteristics. A reputable company or product is something one can trust and believe in to deliver on its promises. The reputation might be based on quality performance, personnel, design, history, or a variety of factors. Perhaps a company has a good reputation for service, treating employees well, continually innovating, or having integrity. A product might have a reputation as being outstanding or superior to competition based on a characteristic. These are typically fact-based belief systems that, at the very least, allow people to believe in something and, at the most might compel people to admire or place a product or company in esteem. A powerful reputation drives value and sales while opening doors and protecting against downside risk. But it can easily be damaged which is why it is wise to help protect a strong reputation with a brand. Remember the Johnson & Johnson Tylenol case mentioned in chapter 7? In some sectors, reputation matters more than others. However, I believe it is essential to understand the reputation you have and, more importantly, the one you want.

Brand: The brand is the complete repository of associations in the mind that are evoked and includes reputational associations. With a powerful brand, the associations often include more symbolic and emotional associations. The brand is a well-designed narrative that informs people on another level and contributes to the reputation. The Johnson & Johnson brand featuring the bond between a mother and child contributes mightily to the reputation of this highly innovative and ethical global diversified healthcare organization. The Apple brand contributes to the reputation of company that has outstanding, market-leading, user-friendly products. The reputation and brand are closely linked, but not the same. There are examples of powerful brands that linked to products or companies with average or below average reputations, or that are trying to shift the reputation. Think about how the Walmart brand—live better by saving more money—contributes to the complex Walmart reputation.

Corporate or Product Identity: This is a rational narrative reflecting how a company describes itself or its products: who it is, what it does, the unique value it brings, and how it can deliver. Sometimes, companies create this corporate or product identity and produce advertising based on it and call that branding. Technically, this is advertising. It may or may not build a powerful brand. Historically, advertising did create brands (see sidebar in chapter 5). Once brands were able to come alive outside of advertising, however, the focus shifted to creating a "brand identity" that could then be delivered across diverse touchpoints, such as customer experience, website, package design, and so on, to create the brand—and it worked. No advertising involved. Powerful brands are built. The corporate identity is not brand strategy, but it serves a useful purpose in helping a company to tell a story in a simple, straightforward, consistent way. It informs the brand, which builds on this foundation, and reflects the reputation.

Reputation, brand, and corporate identity, often used in corporate communications, interact with one another, even though they are separate. A company's reputation may suffer when it is discovered that it has unethical business practices in a foreign country; however, the brand may not be tarnished. Similarly, a brand might become boring and irrelevant, yet not damage a stellar reputation in the near term. Its drag on the reputation will become apparent over time, and the company may need to develop the brand further or rebrand. Typically, the corporate identity does not change much.

The reputation endures yet is always vulnerable—hard to build and easy to topple. If it is properly maintained, that brand also endures; yet it is more fluid as it adapts to the changing culture in order to stay relevant. Together, these three can influence behavior.

In building an Enchanted Brand, we embrace this holy trinity and design the elements not only to work together, but also to contribute value to one another. If for instance, we are starting with a weak reputation that we aim to improve, we take the current state and anticipate the evolution of that reputation in development of the Enchanted Brand.

START WITH THE RATIONAL CORPORATE / PRODUCT IDENTITY.

We begin by distilling the basic narrative of what we are ultimately selling down to: who we are, what we do, the unique value we bring, and the "reason why" to believe? I call this the corporate or product identity. It simply clarifies the value proposition within the market, so it is differentiated and compelling. I like to say it is the "About Us," in that it is the company or product story told from the company's perspective. It is what they want to say or what they want to be heard. The goal is to keep it simple, clear, and logical. The compelling part is the "differentiator of greatest value" which is linked to the most compelling benefit for the purchaser or end user. For example, this is a great-tasting, lactose-free ice cream (unique and compelling differentiator) that allows everyone to enjoy great-tasting ice cream (unique and compelling benefit)—for all the moms buying ice cream who need one kind to please all the mouths, including some lactose-intolerant ones.

Now, this is not as simple as it sounds. Let's take the example above. Someone might believe that the identity should be all about giving lactose-intolerant people a great tasting ice cream. It makes sense. A dominant position in a niche market. However, it misses a key insight. No one wants the stigma of being the "lactose intolerant" kid, no matter how old you are, and the last thing you want to do is highlight the stigma. So, there is a lot of deep listening and empathetic thinking that needs to be done here. I use this work as a strategic platform on which to build the brand. If it is off, the brand doesn't have a chance.

To develop this identity, we use a discovery process. Actually, this process serves development of the corporate identity, brand, and reputational initiatives. It requires diving deep into the sector, competition, buyers, influencers, end users, and relevant trends to figure out the challenges, opportunities, and where you want to end up. What kind of brand do you want? What kind of reputation? More on this process in a bit. Let's stay focused on one of the primary outputs from it—the corporate articles and corporate identity.

CORPORATE ARTICLES

Because the solution we are developing is holistic by design, all elements must be accounted for within it. Sometimes the corporate articles are already established, and it is a matter of aligning them. If not, define them, because they set the basic frame. Volumes have been written on what these are and how to create them, so I'll cut to the chase.

Vision: What is the worldview, driving belief, or visionary outcome that defines why this company or product exists? For example, this company believes mobile technology can democratize knowledge and increase learning capacity and is dedicated to bringing mobile learning to liberate people everywhere to a better way of life.

Mission: What does this company do to accomplish the vision? Maybe it aims to increase access by reducing the cost and distribute it in channels of everyday life. I look at the mission as the "principles of excellence," meaning that the company should measure itself against achieving these. Therefore, the bar should be set high.

Values: In the VUCA world, the moral compass is extremely important as people are highly sensitive and skeptical; remember the chapter on conspiracy theory. Define your values, the kind of company culture you have, and the principles that govern behavior. Here, do not state how you aim to make money or maximize shareholder value. You are explaining your tribe and why people should trust you, believe in you, and support you in good times and bad. This outlines your integrity.

The corporate articles are important to communicate publicly for example, by means of a website, annual report, and other corporate communications as they feed into the reputation and the brand.

CORPORATE IDENTITY

I work with defining four elements to explain the corporate identity.

Who We Serve: Remember, you are not selling. You are serving. Who are the people you aim to please? Doctors, nurses, and mothers? Athletes, coaches, and parents? Use a sentence or two and be descriptive.

Who We Are: This is what some might call the positioning: how do you define what you are? Are you an AI technology company, a health tech company, a health services company, a tech-driven services provider? Nuances matter. Today, we find all kinds of brand-new categories such as a search engine (Google), ride-hailing (Uber) and cryptocurrency (Bitcoin). Do you want to stand alone and create a new category segment? Or do you want to be included in a specific segment? This definition will affect valuation, so think about what the investment community values.

What We Do: This explains what the product or company actually does in simple terms. It doesn't have to be exciting but must be clear. Airbnb is an online vacation marketplace that helps people find and book rental homes using a digital device.

Unique Value We Bring: This is the value proposition. What happens as a result of the "what we do"? Maybe we enable people to afford vacation properties they only dreamed about before. It should be unique. Maybe we deliver the only homey, small-town hospitality experience in New York City. This is what you deliver that no one else does or what you do better than anyone else. What you do best is another way to think about it.

Credibility: This is simply the reason why to believe in the value proposition. It is typically a strategic asset, core competency, or combination of the two. It may be a proprietary technology, uniquely skilled workforce, powerful brand, distribution channel, strategic relationships, or partnerships. This is what makes it real. Even if you have a commodity product, write down what makes it possible. Maybe this company has been in your family for fifty years? That's an asset.

With the corporate articles and corporate identity done, that foundation is set. By the way, this is not a simple process: it requires collaboration, iteration, and crafting. Think about this as the product we are ultimately going to brand. I go through the process for every brand I create even if some of the above elements are already defined. It clarifies the logic. It is important that stakeholders are clear about what these mean and agree on them before beginning to work on the brand. This is the foundation of the branding work. If it is weak or has holes in it, the brand will falter.

The corporate identity is not just a strategic foundation for the brand. It is also used directly in corporate communications.

It may not be emotionally compelling, but is a clear story told in a consistent way. It does not account for how people want to hear the story. It merely states what we want to say—and that, alone, is difficult to pin down.

Remember, this is not the brand. Many companies build a website or create marketing materials based on a corporate identity, which is why they all tend to look the same. It's like wallpaper. Corporate-speak. An ocean of sameness that numbs us all. The company feels good because all the messages are there (and that was hard to do), it "looks professional" and constituents like employees, board members, and investors seem to like it. It is a clear rational narrative that may have some sugar from glossy stock photos and graphic design, but it lacks depth. It wasn't designed to be heard. It can be consistently transmitted but hits a low threshold for meaningful comprehension. Translating this to an audience-centric brand is where exponential value creation occurs.

THE ENCHANTED BRAND PROCESS

The process is analytical, strategic, creative, and holistic. It requires deep insight from digging into the company, market, brandscape, society, culture, and consumers. It requires taking big imaginative leaps to connect the dots in emotionally powerful and intellectually relevant ways. Some of the process includes best practices of traditional branding and other parts pivot into largely unchartered territory where poets and artists live. Most important, it is built from strategic intent. We need a blueprint and that blueprint is the brand strategy.

CHAPTER 8

How the Brand Works

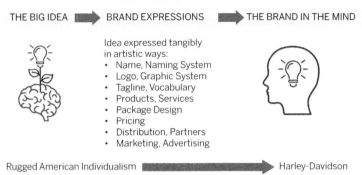

THE BIG IDEA ➡ BRAND EXPRESSIONS ➡ THE BRAND IN THE MIND

Idea expressed tangibly
in artistic ways:
- Name, Naming System
- Logo, Graphic System
- Tagline, Vocabulary
- Products, Services
- Package Design
- Pricing
- Distribution, Partners
- Marketing, Advertising

Rugged American Individualism ➡ Harley-Davidson

As part of the brand strategy, you need to have the following:

1. Key insights, hidden truths, hypotheses
2. Social, cultural trends affecting the consumer and market
3. Brandscape analysis– perceptions about your brand and competitive brands
4. Audience definition and profile--purchasers, users, influencers, employees, stakeholders, the public
5. Reputation assessment--what the reputation is, what created it, what sustains it
6. Corporate identity—definition, vision, mission, positioning, value proposition, credibility (assets, competencies), values
7. Brand imperatives and role—what does the brand need to do?
8. Brand platform—conceptual target, core desire or dream, obstacles, opportunities

Using this strategic platform, you will engage in building a conceptual fabric with one core concept and a supporting structure. The core concept is called the branding idea and is the single, organizing idea of the brand. It delivers on the platform, meets the imperatives, and is tethered to a driving insight or insights. It delivers on what I call the brand scaffold, the elements that hold it up.

The brand scaffolding is: brand vision, brand mission, brand audience, brand promise, brand credibility, brand personality, brand essence, and the branding idea.

Ultimately, this "conceptual" product, which is air-tight with its logic, is summarized in a poetic brand credo which becomes the single, guiding set of principles for building the brand. When these principles are expressed in tangibles and consumed by people, they bring the brand to life in the minds of people.

Although you may long for a prescriptive process, I urge you to be open about the process and look at this as guidelines for a journey. To build an Enchanted Brand, we go beyond traditional branding by doing the following.

Lean Into The Future: Vividly imagine the next five years, next ten. What is that environment going to look like? What will change? How will people change? This is where your Enchanted Brand must operate.

Set Enchantment Goals: Define how this brand will enchant. How will it engage the imagination and get people to think anew? Will it surprise, delight, tickle, soothe, empower?

Discover Enchanted Precedents: Find brands that have at least one element that enchants you and that you'd like for this brand. Get this feedback from employees and target audiences. Maybe the empowerment of Nike or the rule-breaking creativity of Apple are precedents.

Find The Highest Common Denominator: Find the *highest* common denominator between what your product or company can do in the world or for a person and what the person wants and dreams for. *That* is the moment of enchanted connection.

Engage Conceptual Artists And Thinkers: To create artistic and poetic interpretations to help further work the ideas in other realms. This is still part of the strategy process as this is being used to refine the strategic and conceptual platform. Input from scientific researchers, poets, sculptors, designers, gardeners, musicians, and others will be required.

Draw The Brand Trajectory: Enchanted Brands are based on a process of becoming. Draw your brand's brand position today at ground zero, lower left—current perceptions. Draw a star in the far upper right, your brand ideal—what you want this brand to stand for, the ideal perceptions you want to achieve. Draw a line in between and put the brand credo in the middle. When you create brand expressions of principles of the credo, and those expressions are touched and consumed by people, the brand gets built.

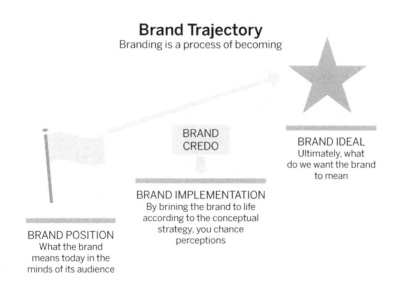

Brand Trajectory
Branding is a process of becoming

BRAND CREDO

BRAND IDEAL
Ultimately, what do we want the brand to mean

BRAND IMPLEMENTATION
By brining the brand to life according to the conceptual strategy, you chance perceptions

BRAND POSITION
What the brand means today in the minds of its audience

REMEMBER DON'T BE LITERAL: THIS KILLS ENCHANTMENT. IT'S ALL ABOUT REFRAMING WITH ENCHANTMENT

Enchanted Brands help people see the world in a new way, through the brand lens. Through Apple, we see technology as the liberator of our inner creativity. Through IBM, the power to process. Brands allow people to interpret products and actions. During the Tylenol crisis, Johnson & Johnson, whose negligence led to the death of several people, was hailed as a saint for removing products from the shelves. Had the brand been Merck, removing products from the shelves would have been seen as the guilty action of a greedy pharmaceutical company. Building a new frame requires understanding the motivations of the target, emphasizing with those motivations by helping them build a new story from the brand perspective. Brands have the power to create an alternative view of a situation as they "treat" reality. They allow people to imagine alternate futures.

CHARACTERISTICS OF ENCHANTED BRANDS

Dare to Be Somebody: Express a clear, distinct point of view, for example, Southwest Airlines.

Convey Premium Brand Quality: Project or infer premium quality, for example, Single Batch Beer.

Are Inspirational: Serve and fulfill dreams, for example, American Idol.

Have a Big Branding Idea: Smile Direct Club—Self-Confidence.

Exceptional, Extraordinary In Some Way: Land Rover is capable of traveling 4,000 contiguous off-road miles.

The Enchanted Brand Identity: The Brand Blueprint.

To build an Enchanted Brand, we create a blueprint. It is a conceptual solution comprised of several principles that, when enacted, build the brand. Think of how the U.S. Constitution and the Bill of Rights bring our democracy to life. The principles are continually interpreted and applied to maintain the republic. In the same way, the Enchanted Brand identity is the blueprint for the Enchanted Brand you aim to create. When actions and objects are expressions of the brand, they bring it to life. They literally transmit the concept to people who consume them—hear them, reach them, experience them. Today, the brand is often delivered in content (for example, social media posts, videos, and podcasts), unique experiences (your Starbucks barista making your specific brew one cup at a time), with communities (lovers of the outdoors getting behind Patagonia), and marketing (advertising, public relations, promotions, and sponsorships). We will talk more about brand building later. In order for all of it to work to build an Enchanted Brand, you need a blueprint.

ENCHANTED BRAND STRATEGY

Knowing our corporate identity, we can now focus on what we need the brand to do. In the Enchanted Brand world, everything is purpose-driven. The brand strategy helps us to define the purpose of our Enchanted Brand.

Business Objectives

What are the business needs requiring brand help? Are we launching a new company, reversing negative sales trends, entering new markets, expanding the product or services line, reinventing, merging or acquiring new assets or capabilities, overcoming a disaster, or simply deciding to more aggressively pursue growth? Identify the brand's value proposition for the business.

Brand Objectives

How do you expect the brand to achieve the business goals? Increase the value or pricing, sharpen the competitive advantage, increase the magnitude of leadership and authority, dispel misperceptions or negative perceptions, or reposition or reframe the company or product? Ultimately, what do you expect the brand to do?

Brand Imperatives

Often, there are obstacles or opportunities we uncover in the discovery process that need to be addressed with the branding solution. Perhaps this is a category of low interest, for example, tires, where we need to pierce indifference? Maybe the technology has a dark side that needs to be gently handled? Perhaps there are words or concepts that should either be avoided or embraced? The brand imperatives section allows you to state the things that must be addressed in order for the brand solution to work.

Brand Audience

Every brand starts with understanding the audience as defined by hopes and dreams rather than demographics or buying profiles. There may be a specific demographic at the heart of your business which your brand will focus on. You are looking to uncover an access point that everyone who consumes your brand will connect to. Maybe it is anxious fathers, people with an inner cheerleader aching to come out, or working mothers who are home-centered providers. These are access points that cut across demographics. Nike originally targeted serious recreational athletes and discovered a universal access point—"unpursued personal ambitions"—that lived inside their core target and everyone: hence, the mass appeal of the brand.

Take some time to identify the groups of people that will consume this Enchanted Brand. Include employees, investors, partners, and local communities. Identify the driving needs, wants, dreams, and fears related to your business and what it does. You'll start to see opportunities to unite them. I call this brand audience the "conceptual target" as it is a conceptual unification that cuts across everyone and unites them.

Unlike marketing, which divides target audiences into groups by needs and wants in order to sell most effectively, the Enchanted Brand audience is about re-massifying the audience to serve them. You are looking for the highest common denominator that cuts across, has meaning for everyone, and unifies. For example, a segment of the market of "single people looking for a mate" may yield a dozen or more groups. The brand, however, must speak to all of them. Maybe, the brand audience will be "pragmatic romantics" or "love givers seeking partners" or "marriage-focused adventures." It all depends on the insights—the hidden, compelling truths—you find in the discovery process which allow you to find a compelling access point. This is how you define the audience for the brand. In doing so, you establish a sandbox right off the bat that the Enchanted Brand must occupy. That's why this exercise should not be taken lightly and requires deep, poetic exploration into the depth of what people hold meaningful.

CORE PRINCIPLES OF THE ENCHANTED BRAND IDENTITY

With the foundation of the corporate identity and the brand strategy, we are now able to design the blueprint. There are six elements to the Enchanted Brand identity, and they are all linked to one big idea—the Enchanted Branding idea. Think of this identity as a diamond in the rough. Every one of these elements that is cutting a facet into this diamond give it shape and value. As you go through the discovery process, you will complete these in your mind.

THE ENCHANTED BRAND IDENTITY

Positioning: What unique conceptual space does it occupy on the brandscape?
Purpose: What does this brand aim to do?
Promise: What unique benefit does the band deliver?
Credibility: What enables the brand to uniquely deliver the benefit?
Personality: What are the humanizing traits of the brand?
Essence: What does this brand stand for?
The Enchanted Branding Idea: What is the big idea that brings all the elements together and speaks to the highest need or want of the brand audience?

You may notice that this structure resembles the corporate identity. What's the difference? The same questions are now being answered from the target audience's perspective. They are conceptual creative rather than strategic. The concepts, language, and emotional design are built around what our audience wants to hear. This is how we translate what you want to say into a language that will be heard. Just like when Hermes (the messenger god who was the son of Zeus and the mountain nymph Maia) translated what the gods had to say so it could be understood (and one of the reasons I named my first brand consulting company Hermeneutics).

THE BIG IDEA: THE BRANDING IDEA

The branding idea is the single galvanizing concept that connects to all elements, answers the demands of the strategy, and defines the structure of the brand. This is the single, organizing principle that combines all of the elements into a compelling, evocative whole. It's the match that ignites the fire of the entire brand blueprint.

The branding idea can come from a number of places. Some find it in the audience (John Deere), others in a culture (Shinola), some in a standard (Pella Window) and others in a promise (Apple). When you go through your discovery process, you'll be searching for the idea. It is the idea that grabs people in their heart. It can be a promise, an aspiration, a goal, a metaphor. It is a concept that speaks to the heart of your conceptual target or a metaphor or truth of great value. I like to think of it as a mind-expanding notion.

Here are a few examples of branding ideas for Enchanted Brands. You may know (some are directly expressed in the tagline):

- The Marines: Many are called. Few are chosen.
- The Army: Be all that you can be.
- The Navy: Join the Navy and see the world.
- Qwest: Ride the light.
- AT&T: Reach out and touch someone.
- Hallmark: When you care enough to send the best.
- Avis: We try harder.
- Ireland: The ancient birthplace of good times.

Note that all of these are not just taglines; they are ideas. They take your mind someplace wonderful and let it wander far behind the reality of the product itself. Some of the best branding ideas never get expressed in a tagline.

Consider the following examples:

- Apple: Genius in creativity, beauty, and life.
- JetBlue: Returning humanity to air travel.
- Starbucks: The Italian coffee-sharing experience.

How can you tell if your branding idea is enchanting? Does it excite you and others? Does it differentiate in an emotional way? Does it help to answer the imperatives and demands of the strategy? Can you easily imagine how it will build value? If you want to explore it further, begin to apply it and create "brand expressions" such as a logo or ad-like objectives. Does it lead to great work? Does that work enchant others?

THE BRAND CREDO: ROSETTA STONE OF BRANDING

The brand credo is the universal brief on brand, the blueprint in words. It is the definitive set of guiding principles that guide behaviors, actions, and applications. It is the tool that employees and vendors use to bring the brand into their line of work.

Like an orchestra that plays many instruments from the same sheet of music, the brand credo ensures that everyone within your organization expresses the brand consistently, whether that applies to product development, promotions, advertising, distribution, pricing, customer service, and everything else the company does. People may decide to express just one fact or several. It is not necessary, and often not possible, to express the entire brand credo in a single thing. Therefore, think about it like an orchestra. Some elements best express one part; other elements another part. Some elements bring it all together into a beautiful symphony.

The brand credo is a condensed version of the blueprint. It

should be simple and moving, and it should contain all core elements needed to express the brand.

There's no static recipe card when it comes to writing a brand credo. You have to feel it and write it to meet the idea. What's important is that the brand credo be short and to the point, and that it knit together all the related elements into a single, moving piece that allows your brand to ring true.

THE DISCOVERY PROCESS

I've mentioned the discovery process quite a bit, so now is a good time to jump into it. What is it? A way for you to explore systematically the cultural and emotional landscape where the Enchanted Brand will operate. When done well, this process should yield insights and guidance for graphic design, marketing, customer experience design, advertising, product design, and innovation.

For the Enchanted Brand, the process veers into the fantasy and the fictional a bit more than the traditional brand discovery process and includes a lot of experiential immersion. It also includes some traditional discovery process elements.

This process should last no less than four weeks and should ideally be twelve to sixteen weeks, depending on the scope and scale of the branding challenge. It's not just the physical time of required to do the work, but the time needed to process and fly with it. It's hard to rush an intellectual and creative marinade.

During this work, we are searching to capture the essence of and find insights about the following: marketing or industry, company, product or service, consumer, culture and competition. Your mission is to boil it down with an eye on the future—what is it now and where is it heading? What's really important to know, and what are the hidden truths that may make a difference? You are now an investigator, a detective. You will find and interrogate all kinds of data, primarily qualitative, observational, and experiential. These the are the primary sources:

1. ***Company Information:*** Reading everything the company has on the market, product, competition and consumer, including research, trend research, history, key memos and speeches that resonated with their listeners, marketing materials past and present. Bathe in it.

2. ***Secondary Research:*** Access analyst, industry, and research reports; use the internet to dig and explore the sector, company, competition, consumers, and trends.

3. ***Primary Research:*** Qualitative research is the bedrock of branding work, because you have to uncover the brand in the minds of people. I conduct focus groups and interviews to listen to (deep listening to comprehend all dimensions of what is being said) prospective customers, current customers, competitive customers, prior customers, influencers, employees, partners, investors, and anyone else who may offer a valuable perspective, such as prior CEOs and leaders, industry experts, the original product inventor, and so on. I like to hear the perspectives both of new employees and veterans, and I have found administrative staff to have great insights.

4. ***Immersions:*** There are lots of fancy names for this, such as ethnographic research. Here, you want to be among "the people" and experience the world that the brand will be activated in with the product. When I was working with the Naval Air Systems Command, my experience on the USS George Washington, an aircraft carrier at sea at an undisclosed location, watching night carrier qualifications[83] gave me the insight behind the branding solution for this complex, diverse organization. This means to place yourself in the environment, open up your heart and mind, jump in and experience it all,

speak with others, and become totally immersed on every possible level. It may require multiple immersions in multiple locations. You decide. Going undercover as a "mystery shopper" for a retail company is a common immersive experience.

5. *Observational:* This differs from immersions in that you are detached and truly observing, looking for patterns and anomalies. You may watch video footage of people using the product. When I worked with ExxonMobil, we took hours of videos watching people pull into an Exxon station, pump gas—how long did it take? who did it? what did they do while it was pumping?—and use the location for a host of reasons, from buying coffee to getting directions and using the restrooms. The patterns informed us about customers' needs, wants, and emotional states.

6. *Literary Review:* This may seem old-fashioned, but this is where you dive off the deep end into books. Could be poetry, fiction, historical. Looking back, I've tended to fall into reading a book or two on every assignment I've had, which both inspired and informed the deeper aspects of the work. This is more of a "feel" decision and is where you will find links to enchantment. You might find it in a children's book. You are letting your intuition and instinct guide you here. Do not fight it. Just go where is sends you and explore. You'll be surprised by the connections you make and the ideas that emerge.

There are more things you can do. Feel free to design your own discovery process that fits the unique demands of your challenge. I'm giving you the basics. If you do these, you'll find what you need to create an Enchanted Brand.

As you go through the discovery process, here are several areas that are helpful to focus on and some tools to use.

WHAT BUSINESS ARE WE IN?

One of the biggest questions to answer in the discovery process is, "What kind of business are we in?" Are you a business that sells crayons, or are you a business that unleashes the colorful creativity of people? If it's the latter, perhaps crayons are just one expression of your business, along with wallpaper, paint, and other products bearing your brand. If you're AT&T, are you a telephone company or a communications company? If you're Nike, are you a sneaker company or a sports company? These definitions set expectations and shape how people will experience your organization as you recast your brand.

For example, when Exxon hired me to evaluate its brand, I came to understand that people were living an ever-greater part of their lives in their cars, that life in the car was emotionally charged, and that this mobile environment came with its own unique set of needs. From this, I developed the idea that it wasn't enough for Exxon just to be in the business of selling gasoline at the retail level; it needed to center its business around meeting the primary needs of drivers on the road—essential and comfort needs. Exxon needed to recast itself within this broader framework. Once we reconceptualized the business, we realized that Exxon's competitors weren't just other oil companies. The competition was also fast food restaurants, convenience stores, and other retail outlets where drivers stopped along their route. By defining itself more broadly, Exxon was better able develop a stronger retail offering that led to higher gasoline sales.

UNDERSTANDING THE BRANDSCAPE

This isn't a traditional competitive analysis. The emphasis is on the brand, not a marketing communications audit. People do not make decisions in a vacuum; they constantly compare your brands in the marketplace. Therefore, it's important to gain a deep understanding of the environment in which your brand operates and the brands in that ecosystem. Does the brandscape consist of many established brands or a series of lesser-known brands? Is there one brand that dominates the market, or several vying for the number one position? Is it sleepy or disruptive? How is the brandscape changing and what are the themes and ideas owned by the brand? You will uncover this information using qualitative research, especially focus groups.

I like to hold focus groups and interviews with employees, partners, employees of competitors, customers, potential customers, influencers, and the media. In addition, we usually complete a communications audit to understand how the competition is trying to portray its brands. Note that the messages they want to get out about their brand often differ greatly from how that brand actually exists in the minds of people. Still, learning these messages is important because it helps to identify the direction in which the competition is trying to push its brands. At the end of the brandscape analysis, you should have a clear picture of the category in which your brand competes, as well as the direction in which competitive companies are trying to take their brands.

One last note. Your buyers may not see the competitive landscape the way you do. Give them to the opportunity to tell you about the alternatives to your product or company. You may be surprised by what they say.

BRAND ARCHEOLOGY

This is particularly relevant for anyone doing rebranding. Here, you need to dive into the minds of the people that matter most and find out what your brand looks like.

Your brand is a composition of associations—ideas, beliefs, attributes, benefits, feelings, and attitudes. Uncovering the associations your brand conjures up in the minds of people is highly interpretive work that requires the ability to fill in the missing pieces to complete the entire brand puzzle.

Assessing a brand is an investigative process. Brands are concepts that reside in people's memories. Unearthing the brand associations requires digging through the minds of people to discover the various pieces scattered about. You have to mine for these associations and piece them together to develop a complete picture of the brand you have. Qualitative research—focus groups and interviews—is the primary tool. Look at chapter 10 for research tools and techniques.

DESIGNING THE ENCHANTED BRAND BLUEPRINT

With the discovery process completed, you can now complete the design of your Enchanted Brand blueprint. You are using inductive reasoning here, the opposite of deductive reasoning. Inductive reasoning makes broad generalizations from specific observations. Basically, you have data and make conclusions from the data. This is called inductive logic. Or you may be using abductive reasoning. You are making and testing hypotheses using the best information available. This process often entails making an educated guess after observing a phenomenon for which there is no clear explanation. My point is that is where art lifts off from science.

This is a highly creative process. There's no how-to guide you can simply fill out. Developing an Enchanted Brand involves exploring metaphors, abstract concepts, and logical literary bridges that are made, destroyed, and remade over again until you achieve a holistic concept that works. Hopefully, inspiration will hit you along the way during your discovery process. This work requires a conceptual thinker with real imagination, who intuitively understands people. Although aspects of this work can be collaborative, this is largely a solitary endeavor. Even if you had access to the most talented poets, would you put them together in a room to write a great poem or would you inspire them to create individually? I have found working with thought partners to be extremely useful. The discovery process was designed to collect input; now the brand creator must use that input to design the blueprint.

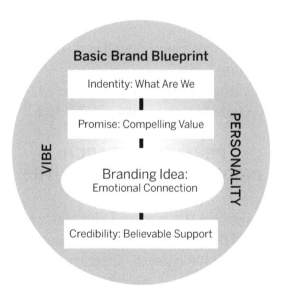

TEN QUESTIONS TO SET YOUR CORPORATE DIRECTION

Corporate directioning involves setting the future direction of your company and establishing the ideal path to take. Here are ten questions to answer in order to determine the corporate direction of your company:

- What business are you really in?
- What are your core competencies and strategic assets?
- What, if taken away, would make your company cease to be what it is?
- What is the sharpest part of your competitive advantage?
- What do you want your company ultimately to become?
- What do you need to get there that is missing?
- What are the trends shaping your industry and how do these affect you?
- What does your company or product do that delights customers most?
- What is the biggest opportunity you have yet to seize?
- How can your brand strengthen people in the VUCA world?

PRIMARY RESEARCH: DIGGING FOR HIDDEN TRUTHS

If there is one thing I have learned after thirty years in branding, it's that all of the important things are never written down. You simply have to talk to people—*really* talk to them. I like to use the format of one-on-one interviews and approach it fresh. Meaning, I don't read too much ahead of time, so I can really hear and listen to what people tell me. The interview is not simply about asking questions but is about "getting into the zone" with the people being interviewed and letting them share their deep thinking. Observe body language and notice what makes them excited. Areas to explore include getting their thinking about and listening to how they explain:

Basic Data
- Core competencies and assets of the company
- Company strengths and weaknesses
- Company's history and future direction
- Feelings about key competitors and threats
- Company culture description
- Feelings about current brand
- Views on competitive companies and their brands?

Dreamscaping
- If you could change one thing about the brand, what would it be?
- What would you do if you were CEO one day?
- What is your ideal description of the company?

Success Factors
- Issues will need to be addressed for branding to succeed
- Hot buttons within the culture
- Who's on board, who's not and why

Brand Purpose is a Driver

According to McKinsey, excellent CEOs spend time thinking about, articulating, and championing the purpose of their company as it relates to the big-picture impact of day-to-day business practices.84 They push for meaningful efforts to create jobs, abide by ethical labor practices, improve customers' lives, and lessen the environmental harm caused by operations. Visible results matter to stakeholders. For example, 87 percent of customers say that they will purchase from companies that support issues they care about, while 94 percent of millennials say that they want to use their skills to benefit a cause, and sustainable investing has grown eighteen-fold since 1995.[85]

TAKEAWAYS

- Reputation, brand, and corporate identity are interrelated, but not the same.
- Enchanted Brands are a form of public service at a time when humanity is vulnerable.
- Enchanted Brands differ from traditional brands in that they engage the imagination and liberate the mind to think outside the box.
- Like poetry, Enchanted Brands engage the imagination and fill the senses, linking the conscious and unconscious.
- Enchanted Brands help people make dreams into reality.
- A deep, robust discovery process fuels development of the Enchanted Brand blueprint.

QUESTIONS TO EXPLORE

- What are the differences between your corporate identity and your brand?
- Think of three examples of Enchanted Brands. Why you find them enchanting?
- What is currently or could be enchanting about your brand?
- Why would you want to create an Enchanted Brand?

9
The Enchanted Brand Gallery

PEOPLE ALWAYS LONG FOR CASES TO ILLUSTRATE OR DECON-
struct in the hopes of illumination and deeper understanding.
I don't believe that will help you here. Just as dissecting a frog kills
it or showing the reality behind a magic trick forever removes the
magic, analysis will take the enchantment out of the examples.
What will be helpful is to stimulate your imagination by sharing
examples of Enchanted Brands and why I find them enchanting. I
do this with the sole purpose of inspiring you to use your imagination and let go. Enchanted Brands are born of inspiration, vision,
and creativity.

I've provided all the guidance and tools you need to create an
Enchanted Brand in previous chapters. Have confidence and don't
look for an explicit process to use as a crutch. You don't need it.
Explore each one of these and let yourself process what it means
to you. Some of these I've worked on, other ones I just admire.
Although I am not explaining the bespoke process behind each
one, you can get to any of these through the guidance I've provided.
What's most important is to allow your mind to wander.

THE ENCHANTED BRAND GALLERY

John Deere
American Farmer Ethos

I've mentioned this brand several times as I'm a big fan. I find
it utterly enchanting. For decades, John Deere has continued to
honor, celebrate, and myth-make the life of the American farmer.
The brand stands for that mystical, captivating down-to-earth,
dirt-on-your-hands ethos. It's not the Marlboro cowboy, but it's

pretty darn close. That's why so many people wear the green hat with the yellow logo and proudly honor the idea that "nothing runs like a Deere," which is a reflection of the people the brand serves: hardworking, nature-loving, full of integrity, can't be beaten, beauty-loving. John Deere means something, stands for something, and evokes a world of farmland horizons and good, down-to-earth people earning an honest living doing something they really love.

Chanel
Feminine Beauty

What Chanel does that is enchanting is to define feminine beauty. The brand has been doing it for decades, globally, and owns the space. By featuring Chanel women from Catherine Deneuve to Kristin Stewart, it finds beautiful women who are evocative and enchanting and makes them accessible to us all. What does it take to be a Chanel woman? What is Chanel beauty all about? The dreamy and aspirational exterior beauty is made intimate and accessible, but just as important is that these women have depth—feminine mystique kind of depth carried by every woman. We are all Chanel women, because we all have this within us. Chanel reminds us and helps us to unleash our feminine beauty—however we want to define it. Chanel, like any good Enchanted Brand, is not prescriptive. It allows you to expand and find your own way, rather than overtly direct you to a specific way. Chanel elevates all women to the enchantment of ultimate feminine beauty.

Patagonia
Outdoor Heaven

There are many outdoor brands, but Patagonia is enchanting because it loves the outdoors in an authentic, beautiful way by elevating the outdoors to the level of a deity. It admires the outdoors and passionately invites everyone to enjoy *and* protect it, because it is so special. It makes the outdoors enchanting and accessible. It brings you in and shows you how to respectfully enjoy all that enchantment without preaching. Patagonia was doing this before social responsibility was a twinkle in anyone's eye. Its catalogs were one of the first to break from featuring products, to featuring something much more important—irresistible beauty of the outdoors and outdoor experiences. This brand enchanted us not just by bringing us to beautiful places, but by showing us a beautiful way to experience them.

National Geographic
Adventure and Exploration

This 130-year-old brand continues to enchant the world through its mission of exploration and discovery. It has 72 million social media followers.[86] Although it has scientific roots, it has always made science accessible and invited people into its wide and deep explorations from outer space to under the sea to urban and mountain cultures to—you name it. It is like a land rover that knows no boundaries and takes us along for the ride—safely. Like a strong Enchanted Brand, it has integrity and never exploits. You know it is trying to help you feel something and see something important, and often feel it has taken great risks to do so. The unrelenting exquisite quality comes from a deep passion to discover deeply and share enchanting aspects of all that exists. One might say this brand exists purely to enchant.

Qwest
Ride The Light

I worked on this brand which transformed itself from a small fiber optic construction company owned by Phil Anschutz into the country's-fourth largest telecom in just eighteen months with just over $1 million in marketing. The idea behind "Ride the Light" was about harnessing the enchanting and provocative power of light to usher in a new age of fast, error-free communications that would free people to enjoy a new level of adventure. People were enchanted by the notion that light was now taking over in telecom, from the dark, domineering grip of the previous big three telecoms, and that riding it to wherever it would take them would be a thrilling experience. This brand was credited with producing the meteoric success of Qwest.

Johnson & Johnson
Bond Between Mother and Child

This is arguably the most trusted brand in the world. The trust links to its single-minded focus on the bond between a mother and child. That bond is universal, pure, and stands for absolute, unconditional love. Everyone understands that bond. As one of the world's largest, diversified pharmaceutical companies, Johnson & Johnson grabbed that idea and works hard to keep it alive. They also always positioned themselves as a healthcare rather than a pharmaceutical company. Rather than showing labs and white coats, they showed mothers and babies. By leveraging the powerful bond of unconditional love between a mother and child, it was able to tap symbolically into big themes like innocence, purity, vulnerability, and trust. This is one of the most sophisticated brand strategies I have ever seen, and it is enchanting in its simplicity and authenticity. This corporate brand brings uncontested trust to the two-hundred-plus parent companies under its umbrella and delivers real value.[87]

American Express
Travel-Related Services

I mention this brand because it may not feel enchanting at first. You have to marvel at the brilliance of a financial services company grabbing the glamor of travel for its brand and making it work. American Express is a company that processes financial transactions. It moves money around. Yet, the brand is all about the glamour and adventure of travel—travel-related services. Mastercard tried to counteract this strategy with its "priceless" brand strategy, but the American Express ownership of travel and all that it brings is unassailable. Like you, I find travel to exotic places to be enchanting.

Orvis
Refined Outdoor Recreation

Orvis is a fictional fairy tale of a "gentlemen's approach" to fly-fishing and wing shooting. There is a distinct point of view about how to enjoy and master these pursuits while maintaining a level of relaxed sophistication and a pedigree of refinement and aristocratic recreation. This world not only has equipment and vacation destinations but breeds of dogs that go with it. For anyone who wants to disappear into a gentile world of outdoor recreation, no one enchants like Orvis.

DÔEN
The Female Collective

This new fashion brand born in 2017 broke all the rules and has quickly created a global "collective" of followers that makes Apple fans look tame. You can spot a DÔEN woman on the street in an instant. Imagine a fashion brand in Los Angeles flying right over the domineering fashion houses of New York City and Milan to introduce a distinctive feminine lifestyle—100 percent online. It came from a real need: west coast women wanting different fabrics and a softer feel. DÔEN works because of its brand. It's for women who have a soft yet strong sensuality and enjoy simple, natural, beauty in life and the world. The thoroughly modern ideal is inclusive and allows anyone to become part of the collective and join in the spirit. Like all Enchanted Brands, it does not prescribe or dictate—it invites and allows personal expression. It passionately and generously shares all that it finds enchanting This brand has a strong voice and worldview that goes to all the issues of our time, always bringing the gentle and firm DÔEN integrity. They might just be clothes, but it sure feels like a fairy tale to me.

Apple
Empower Your Creativity

No Enchanted Brand list would be complete without this brand which makes technology into the ultimate creative empowerment tool. That was bold. Apple has superior ease of use, great design, outstanding processing abilities—yet the brand went elsewhere. It invited you to open up your creative self, to produce and enjoy more creative content. And it elevated this to a high aesthetic and an aspirational and youthful way of life for businesses, individuals, schools, nonprofits—everyone. Apple became a brand to help you change your life and the world. The products made it easy. Break the rules, think different—don't be a lemming. Don't miss out on the life you can create. It made computers and home technology enchanting and it still does.

Nike
Pursue Your Passion

Aside from Apple, Nike is the other ultimate Enchanted Brand. Nike also had a superior product that helped people perform better in sports. However, the brand went beyond to personal empowerment. It stood for *carpe diem,* pursue your passion. Get your drive on, push your ambition and go. Doesn't matter if you win or finish. It's all about just doing it. This permission and encouragement resonated with an achievement-driven culture that needed to be freed from outcomes and allowed to just get into action. I witnessed people go from owning one pair of sneakers to owning over ten. Many would never run a mile, but with Nike they were part of the fitness revolution, empowered to feel their inner athlete, and emboldened to go do things they've always wanted to do. Not too bad for a sneaker company. This brand would allow that little sneaker company to dominate and then move into every single category of sports equipment and apparel over time, even into such places as golf and football that were locked and inaccessible.

Naval Air Systems Command
Reign Supreme, Return In Glory

I worked with the Naval Air Systems Command in 2001 and started the day after 9/11. This technology command over the past decade had turned into an innovation powerhouse whose products were advancing all services, not just the Navy. However, its brand was rooted in history. The rebranding focused on what NAVAIR was able to bring to warfighters in the field. With excellence in naval aviation technologies, it delivers the ultimate power in combat and the ultimate safety. When translated into a brand, that meant "Reign Supreme and Return in Glory," which became enchanting words that changed the world for NAVAIR. Some 200 admirals gave a standing ovation when they saw the brand and it gave all warfighters a new view and kinship with it. Adm. Joseph Dyer, the four-star in charge of NAVAIR, said of the brand, "It was a real surprise. It brought us all together, even the warfighter, on a common emotional path."

The New York Times
Truth

During the tumultuous Trump administration, when the press came under unrelenting attack and violent scrutiny with an intention of undermining its authority, this newspaper rolled out its brand. This brand stands for what all great journalism seeks: truth. It invites everyone in to embrace what it takes to go after and report the truth—which is not easy. It takes courage, curiosity, stamina, integrity and strength to not back down. It is so enchanting it makes me want to be courageous. *The New York Times* brand reaches the inner journalist within each of us to be courageous. This brand reminds us of how important it is to have people working to find and share the truth and speaks to our sense of integrity. It elevates the conversation and provokes us to think deeply.

Black Rifle Coffee
Military Grade Brew

The military has its own level of enchantment which comes to life with this brand. Created by veterans who also hire and support veterans, the brand digs into the masculine, gritty, no-kidding culture of military life. Black bags, rifles, flavors such as Freedom Roast. It makes you think of drinking coffee around a campfire somewhere with compadres, on a mission to defend this great country of ours and uphold duty and honor. I'm all in.

I could go on and include brands like Jeep (adventure), Corona (I'll take that beach) and Ralph Lauren Polo. What's interesting to me is why brands that were once enchanting, stopped. AT&T, McDonald's, and Coca-Cola, to name just a few, once held our hearts and pushed our imaginations. Not anymore. It's all about clever advertisements and marketing promotions. That's our loss. Enchanted Brands really care about their customers, which is why they enchant. They contribute to the culture at large in ways that make a difference. We all need more of that today.

TAKEAWAYS

- Enchanted Brands have big ideas and don't need to come from big companies.
- Enchanted Brands don't prescribe, they stimulate the imagination.
- Enchanted Brands create worlds and make them accessible.

QUESTIONS TO EXPLORE

- Create a list of five brands that are enchanting to you. Explore what makes them enchanting.
- Can you think of any brands that used to enchant and no longer do?

10

Rebranding To Become Enchanted

---

*"I can't believe that!" said Alice. "Can't you?" the Queen
said in a pitying tone. "Try again: draw a long breath
and shut your eyes." Alice laughed. "There's no use
trying," she said, "one can't believe impossible things."
"I daresay you haven't had much practice," said the
Queen, "When I was your age, I always did it for half-
an-hour a day. Why sometimes I've believed as many as
six impossible things before breakfast."*
—Lewis Carroll, Alice in Wonderland[88]

SUSPECT THAT THIS MAY BE THE MOST IMPORTANT CHAPTER,
because most people are interested in rebranding, instead
of creating a new brand. First, if you have a brand, don't think
about throwing it away and starting over with a spanking new
brand unless it has so much negative equity that it must retire.
It is hard to build brand awareness and equity. Once you have
it, you don't want to throw it away. Even if perceptions are not
exactly what you want them to be, it is easier to shed and build
new perceptions on an existing foundation than to start from
ground zero with something new. For example, when US Air had
multiple planes falling out of the sky, the brand evolved with a
new name—US Airways—and an emphasis on safety. We trans-
ferred the positive equities (there are always some) and added
new ones, and the rebranding was highly successful in supporting business growth.

Rebranding is not easy. Even a billion-dollar brand such as Weight Watchers can get it wrong. In 2019, after spending millions of dollars and over a year on an intensive rebranding solution, the company relaunched with a new brand. Yes, they threw away their category-dominant brand. Why would you toss out a valuable brand? Clearly someone thought that brand was an albatross and had no value. I cannot imagine how this happened. The new brand has a new name—WW. No more Weight Watchers, which is a shame, because that was actually a brilliant name. The new brand is no longer about weight loss, the very essence of a brand that dominated the category for decades. It owned the category-dominant promise—weight loss. The new brand is all about wellness. The dominant name in weight loss, the uncontested big boy, traded its huge equity "weight loss" for "wellness." Sigh. They launched the rebrand with disastrous results. The stock plummeted, consumers got confused, sales dropped, and things went sideways quickly. There has been rumors that this misstep is under reconsideration. I mention this as a cautionary tale, that even bright minds with big investments can get it wrong. Do *not* overthink this. Stay close to the authentic dreams and desires of the people you are serving. Weight loss may be simple, but that does not make it unenchanting. You have to put the enchantment into it.

When people want to rebrand, usually it is because they know something is wrong with their brand. Sometimes, people tell them their brand is weak or messed up or the sales and marketing team report chronic issues. Sometimes, leaders see the writing on the wall that suggests their brand is eroding. Other times, big new brand competition enters into the industry, causing a reassessment. In addition, some want to be more aggressive, gain more market share, move up to premium pricing, or enter new markets. There are times when rebranding happens simply to improve valuation. It's important to identify the business reasons why are "considering" evolving your brand. Why are you exploring this and what do you hope to gain? Also, think about "who" needs to think and feel "what" to make your goals happen. Identify the perceptual, intellectual, and emotional barriers that stand in your way as well as the cracks, openings and opportunities for success. Use the discovery process in chapter 6.

Remember, perception is reality. Once you know the perceptions and emotions you want to eliminate and the ones you want to create, then you can begin to design your Enchanted Brand.

Brand Re-Positioning Examples

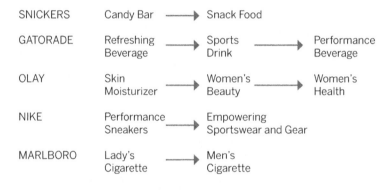

THE ROADMAP: THE REBRAND TRAJECTORY

As mentioned, branding is a process of becoming. Brands are always in motion and are context-sensitive. We want to put your brand on a path to an ideal destination. I call this the brand trajectory. One point on the trajectory is the brand position which defines where you brand is today and why. The second point is the brand ideal. This defines where your brand aims to end up and what it aims to become. In an ideal world, what people would have in their minds about your brand. These two points create the broad path, a direction.

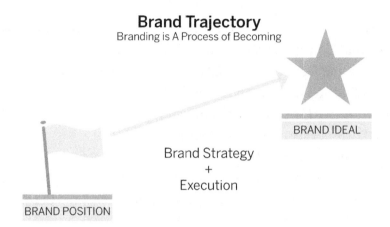

Brand Trajectory
Branding is A Process of Becoming

BRAND IDEAL

Brand Strategy
+
Execution

BRAND POSITION

To move from the brand position to the brand ideal, you need to take consistent actions guided by your Enchanted Brand blueprint (see chapter 8). Those actions create touchpoints that create the brand in people's minds. This is your simple map for evolving your brand to an Enchanted Brand state.

KNOW WHAT YOU HAVE

Step one is to get to know your brand really well. As mentioned in chapter 8, your brand is all of the associations, beliefs, ideas, and emotions that are in people's minds and that are evoked when they are exposed to a brand signifier—name, logo, package, smell, and sound. You will want to explore how your brand exists in the minds of people—employees, customers, target customers, partners, investors, journalists, analysts, and for some, even the general public. Now, your brand may exist differently with different segments of people, and that is worth knowing as it will guide your engagement strategies. I call this doing a brand assessment, and I cannot overstress the importance of doing this and doing it well. Most likely, you will be surprised by some of what you discover.

Many people I meet say they have done an analysis of their brand and competitive and peer brands. Then, they show me an analysis of marketing messages, websites, and advertising. This shows us how companies are communicating about their brand, which is important, but it does not tell us how the brand exists in the mind. For that, you must do primary qualitative research with key communities. I call it brand archeology. You are digging into the conscious and unconscious to discover how the brand exists. Unfortunately, asking brand questions directly doesn't work. In fact, it can give you false data. Because the brand is not attached entirely to rational thinking and lives in the memory, it is hard for people to explain any brand and how they really relate to it. It is your job to go into the mind and find it. Here are some tools you can use to do some of your own brand archeology (see sidebar for details on each):

Brand Assessment Tools

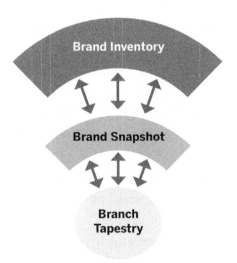

- **Brand Inventory:** Elicit every word that comes to mind when someone thinks about a brand by asking, "When I say (brand name), you think..." and let them fill-in the blank until they have no more words.

Brand Inventory Example: Outdoor Water Container Brand

ACTIVITIES	HYDRATION	HYDRATION SYSTEM
Hiking	Water	Hard to clean
Biking	Water only	Hands free
Outdoors	Refreshing	Water backpack
Camping	Thirst	Bite to drink
Running	Water storage	
Skiing	Easy way to hydrate	
Outdoorsey		

ATTRIBUTES		PEOPLE	EXPENSIVE	OTHER
Quality	Cooling	Hikers	Pricey	Endurance
Rugged	Necessity/Essential	Bikers	A luxury	Desert
Lightweight	Easy	Families	Costs too much	Camel
Comfortable	Clever	Climbers	Costly	Safety
Functional	Innovative	Marines		Fun
Reliable	Convenient	Special Ops		On the Go
Good Design	Versatile			Adventure
	Multi-purpose			

- *Brand Snapshot:* Ask people to describe or draw a single image that best captures the brand.
- *Brand Tapestry:* Provide twenty-five to thirty-five symbolic/emotional photographs and ask people to use them to construct their view of the brand by placing the most important images in the center and least important on the periphery.

When doing these exercises, listen deeply and observe the process. Are the brand associations deep or shallow? Was this work hard or easy for people to do? What was the energy like? Was it fun and animated or quiet and stressful? Listen to the casual dialogue. Put these findings together to draw insights about the category, your brand, and the competition. This is also part of the assessment.

There are other tools you use, but I find these three sufficient to unearth the data needed to assess a brand and its competition fairly. It is important to assess the competition not only to understand brand structure, strengths, and weaknesses, but also because people make decisions in a relative framework. They choose by comparing one option against another. You want to understand the comparative brand dynamic. Choose competitive brands that allow you to understand the primary comparisons being made in a purchase decision. If you are not sure, you can do a simple exercise where you ask people, using qualitative research, about their decision-making process and the brands within it. Ask them to name and categorize the brands in their mind. I find this to be an extremely valuable exercise and sometimes it can be surprising. When I construct the brand assessment work, I usually keep it to three or four brands at most.

After you collect your data, it's time for analysis. Answer the following to complete it.

BRAND ASSESSMENT

- *Brand Definition:* This is where you meet your brand. What are *all* of the associations that come to mind? Separate them into conceptual groups. Maybe there are associations linked to the product? Linked to history? Linked to the company? Linked to an idea? Also, note which associations are the most or least important; I often assign a ranking. Plot them all on a map showing strength and conceptual groupings. You can use various research tools with the data to help you make it more analytical, or just create a visual that tells the story as you see it. This is your brand, naked.

7. ***Brand Equity:*** Identify all of the positive associations, ones that have value. Again, these should be rated and ranked. Also, if you can, trace back to what is creating these associations, the touchpoints that are responsible for them. Is it the product experience? Packaging? What others say? Advertising? These are the perceptions you want to keep, and some may be ones you want to build on depending on where you want to go with your brand and what will have traction in the world.

8. ***Brand Liabilities:*** Identify the negative associations and perform the same exercise as above. These are the perceptions that you want to neutralize or eliminate. Try hard to find the root sources and what sustains them, as this will be important when you act to neutralize or eliminate them.

9. ***Conceptual Structure:*** What is the idea holding all of these elements together? Now, there may be a weak brand structure meaning there is no "big idea" at work, and we just have a bunch of associations. You may find a simple idea, such as, "This is the biggest pharmaceutical company in the world," which creates a lot of associations. Or it may be a creative idea, such as, "This is the beer to bring to the beach with friends," which drives a lot of the equities.

10. ***Key Attributes and Beliefs:*** I like to link these associations to beliefs people carry. Maybe there is deep trust or distrust. Maybe they believe this brand will have answers about the future or makes the world a better place. Maybe they want to share this brand with others and are advocates or they feel it is on a downward spiral. In this section, you are identifying conclusions that people make about the product or company form the brand.

Brand Assessment Elements: Examples

EQUITIES (KEEP)	LIABILITIES (REMOVE)	BELIEFS
High-quality	Getting outdated	Feels old-fashioned
Trustworthy	Not exciting anymore	Not confident it will be here
Reliable service	Losing its way	long
Made in Italy	Not modern enough	No vision for the future
Hand-crafted	Seems like it is cheapening	Doesn't care about the
Always delivers		community
Stands behind its word		

Depending on your business and what you find, you may want to add other elements, but this covers the basics. It is easy to get lost in a brand assessment because the process is so exciting. There is often a tendency to want to overshare the insights and information. Most people just want you to cut to the chase. Therefore, I report the data in a simple format called a brand audit (see below) and provide access to executive summaries and detailed reports for those who have an interest to learn more.

Brand Audit Template

"Phrase that captures what most people would say about the brand"

Photograph Representing The Primary Visual of the Brand	PRIMARY BRAND ASSOCIATIONS	BRAND EQUITIES	BRAND LIABILITIES
	Words/phrases most frequently said about the brand, typically a list of 10-12 with the most highlighted	The list of brand associations that bring value	List of brand associations that detract value

	BRAND BELIEFS	BRAND EMOTIONS
	What people said they believe about the brand including what I can and cannot do	The emotions that came to mind when people thought about the brand

Statement Of The Challenge Facing The Brand

ASSESS BRAND POWER

Before you begin to develop your brand, you need to measure and understand its power. The example above provided a sense of brand strengths and weaknesses, but it did not allow us to understand deeply the elements that make a brand powerful. This is important as you move out to change your brand and develop it in a meaningful way. I like to understand brand power by looking at ten standard brand power measures and sometimes add other "attribute" power measures which may be relevant in driving value in a specific business industry, such as innovation, creativity, craft mastery, financial acumen, and so on. I collect data on brand power using quantitative research, a survey of questions using a ten-point scale (answer on a scale of one to ten) except for measure number one, brand awareness. Many of these are composite measures, meaning there are multiple questions (maybe two to four) providing data points that are aggregated, ideally on a weighted basis, to yield the score for the measure.

Brand Power Measures

1. ***Brand Awareness:*** Measured on an unaided basis (when you think of x business, what brands come to mind?) and aided basis (have you ever heard of this brand?). This is where your brand actually exists. If a person has never heard of your brand, it does not exist for them. Maybe your brand exists in 10 percent of the minds you want to reach?

2. ***Brand Affinity:*** Aside from awareness, this is the single greatest determinant of success. How strong is the emotional connection with the brand?

3. Brand Likeability: Related to the above, yet different. Sometimes people have a strong connection with a brand, but they don't love it. Here, we want to know how much they like the brand, which allows us to see the level of enthusiasm and advocacy.

4. Brand Differentiation: How unique is this brand in its category? This helps to understand the magnitude of difference. Are you in a sea of sameness or standing apart?

5. Brand Clarity: This measures how well people feel they understand the brand and if there is any confusion or conflict which needs to be cleared up.

6. Brand Authenticity: This measures the degree to which a brand has a sense of truth, real, or pure intention, a genuine and clear point of view.

7. Brand Integrity: Does this brand have character, operate with a moral compass, have a desirable value system?

8. Brand Esteem: How much does a person hold this brand in high regard? Perhaps this brand is a well-respected gatekeeper or thought leader.

9. Brand Relevance: I like to ask people not about how relevant the brand is to them (this is clear from answers to the other questions), but how relevant they feel the brand is in culture today. It is important in the world? Does it make a difference?

10. Brand Momentum: I like to know if people see this brand as moving up, sliding back, or holding steady, because brands are always in motion. What kind of energy is behind your brand?

11. Brand Purpose: I added this eleventh measure to reflect that people today want brands that make the world a better place. Therefore, it is helpful to know where your brand and the competition sits.

I like to assess brand power across multiple groups and compare and contrast the results to find insights. Minimally, this should be conducted among current and prospective purchasers and influencers on the purchase decision which includes end-users. If budget permits, I like to include stakeholders (employees, leadership, investors), competitors (in case they have a different view), and experts (such as cleaning ladies for cleaning brands). This diverse input helps provide insight on the dimensions driving power and value.

Brand Power Data Analysis Example

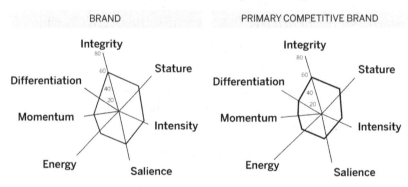

Both the brand assessment and brand power scorecard combined with the discovery process (see chapter 6), will allow you to understand fully where your brand is today and why and what it needs. At this point, you should know what you want to keep about your brand and what you want to lose. Now, we need to figure out where your brand needs to go.

HOW TO DEFINE YOUR BRAND IDEAL

The brand you are creating is not happening in the past or the present. It is happening in the future and will operate years into the future. Therefore, you have to read the tea leaves of the future to understand the context surrounding your brand and figure out what kind of brand it needs to be for success. It surprises me that many people do not take this step in rebranding, especially in a VUCA world. This is why some rebrands lose relevance before they are even launched. They failed to align with the changing world. Knowing about the VUCA world, new essentialism, the leaning toward conspiracy theory, and the highly volatile nature of the human side of business today, you know a lot. That's a very good start. I also encourage you to conduct your own trend research as there are many accessible sources from sources including Trend Hunter, Culture Vulture, and Sparks & Honey. Think about your business, you customer, and the culture. What will the future look like for your brand? How will it be different from today? How might this affect your brand? Many companies will commission custom studies to understand the future of work, the future of masculinity, the future of love, or any future state that will affect their brand and business. They use those insights to fine-tune their brand and business moving into the future.

Now, you need to think as an idealist and put yourself into the future. Imagine all the words, feelings, and beliefs you want people to say when they hear your brand in the future—and why. What are the thoughts, feelings, and beliefs that are going to create the value your company needs in the future? Don't restrict yourself to just naming a list of attributes. Put down exactly what you want people to say when they hear or see your brand name. I admit, this process can be challenging. However, if you understand the future world—your human side of business, your industry and competition, and the culture—it will be clear. This requires a leap of imagination to connect the dots with an "if this, then that" mindset. You have to claim a star in the sky to steer by. You have everything you need to do it.

Once you have created the "brand ideal," then you should compare it with your brand position, that is, where your brand is today. This will allow you to uncover a series of transitions that need to occur in your rebranding. For this, you may draw upon insights from your discovery process. I have found identifying these transitions to be extraordinarily useful in explaining the path of rebranding and extremely valuable in implementing it. Again, this "brand transformation" guide comes from analyzing where you are today with where you want to be in the ideal world and imagining the changes that need to occur.

People often ask me how long it will take to achieve the brand ideal. My answer is always the same: does it really matter? The brand ideal is a star to steer by, a destination to which to aspire. It is not the actual thing we are doing to get there. Implementing the principles of the brand credo with passion and consistency is what matters. That is what creates new brand value. To figure out those principles and the big idea, we need to understand the path from brand position to brand ideal. Even if we don't achieve the brand ideal, the path is exactly what we need to be doing to get there. That path—driven by the brand identity and captured in the brand credo—is what delivers the enchanting brand. Now that you have defined the trajectory for the rebranding, let's figure your Enchanted Brand identity.

PUTTING ENCHANTMENT INTO YOUR BRAND

Through this process, you have identified what perceptions you want to keep, to lose, to add, and to emphasize in your rebranding. This part of the process is super important. You cannot believe how many people fail to do this fundamental work before launching into crafting their rebrand identity. This should be articulated in your brand imperatives, brand trajectory and supporting brand transitions. Together, these set the parameters for the rebranded, enchanted identity.

Now, you are going to follow the same process provided in chapter 8. To add some sparks, here are some suggestions to stir your imagination, intuition, and creativity further. Remember, Enchanted Brands are illusions that endure and live in the real world. Unlike traditional brands, they are designed to serve rather than sell and to engage the imagination in order to liberate new thinking and empower. They aim to merge intellect with imagination in a cognitively-immersive experience that allows a person to see the world from the Enchanted Brand view and participate in that world. To create this kind of brand, we need an empathetic understanding of how it is going to operate and resonate with impact and agency.

A DEEP LISTENING APPROACH

As described in chapter 8, this is an opportunistic and entrepreneurial process. It aims to find or create openings from which to create specific value by examining the questions, puzzles, and enigmas that are inherent in humanity, its behaviors, composition, sentiments, and thoughts. As brand creators, we see the world full of opportunities to create ideas that can have impact and new concepts that can influence the way people see, think, feel, act, and behave.

This form of inquiry differs from scientific inquiry and analytical problem-solving. Enchanted Branding is more concerned with framing questions that expand how we understand and think about a problem from multiple perspectives to uncover multiple pathways forward. These perspectives and pathways are associated with values and beliefs—the frames through which people engage with the world. Through an iterative process, we pose and reframe questions, explore ideas under multiple terms, and recalibrate. We work to understand the relationships between people, cultural frames, actions, thinking, feeling, and contexts. We are looking for the opportunity make meaning that can influence actions, thinking, and feelings.

This approach requires asking really good questions and listening deeply. You want to interrogate the consumer psyche, the market dynamics, the competition and ecosystem, the future, and emergence aggressively. Free yourself to bring in others or create new methodologies to open questions. Tap networks of partners and diverse "thinking" resources in an energetic exchange process. As brand creators, we are focused on ideas that bring action and agency. We aim to create disturbances in the environment— some of no significance and others with capacity for impact.

The Enchanted Brand intertwines action and thinking. Branding is thought through creative action. As the revered intellectual poet Octavio Paz said in his essay on "The Poetry of Solitude and the Poetry of Communion," there are two ways of being in the world. One is the warrior way and the other is the mystic.[89] The warrior way aims to dominate, subjugate, and conquer reality through knowledge and power. The warrior is separate from the world, an agent operating on it. The mystic, on the other hand, wants to become immersed in reality and understand it rather than control it. The mystic is comfortable with questions, no answers, and ambiguity. The warrior pursues action, the mystic pursues understanding. The warrior is aggressive and the mystic is empathetic. Enchanted Branding is the mystic.

FIND PRECEDENTS

These can be mental vehicles of play to avoid blank-mind paralysis, unproductive looping of linear thinking, and to put your free-play imagination into motion. A precedent is an example of something that was previously done. Unlike a legal precedent, you are going to look for precedents that are related to the work you are doing so that you can assimilate what others have done and inspire your imagination. Approach precedents opportunistically, looking for things that can be useful. Maybe you are inspired by the bootcamps of Facebook, the single cup brewing process of Starbucks, or how food trucks bring restaurants to the customer rather than having customers come to the restaurants. Look for pieces. Precedents are a great way to get started.

IMMERSION

Over my career, this has always where I have found my greatest inspiration, unspoken truth, and the kindling for novel ideas. On the deck of the George Washington at sea watching carrier qualifications at two in the morning for NAVAIR. Packing pizzas in a Godfather's Pizza store with employees and serving customers. Being among families and their children at the Boston Children's Hospital. I seem to always find my answers by just letting go and deeply immersing myself in the context—in the environment. Minimally, it always helps me to connect the dots and discover things I never considered. During this intense state of being where I absorb, exchange, and observe, I discover a new way of seeing and being in the brand's context. I also find it to be personally enriching and expanding. Think about how and where to immerse yourself.

WORLD BUILDING

This is a novel tool developed by Alex McDowell, professor at the University of Southern California's School of Cinematic Arts and Director of the World Building Media Lab.[90] It helps to set the imagination in motion. World building first appeared in literature next in the 1970s science fiction, and then in film *(Minority Report, The Matrix, Avatar, Lord of the Rings, Chronicles of Narnia, Harry Potter, and Star Wars)* and game design *(Dungeons and Dragons, World of Warcraft)*. Building worlds has a history that dates back to Charles Dickens, James Joyce in *Ulysses,* and Lewis Carroll's *Alice in Wonderland.* Building worlds engages the imagination, allows things to happen differently and for us to understand the why and how—which leads to new meaning.

World building is a process of engineering a fictional world. World building starts with an expansive propositional question. It asks "What if" something is possible and then constructs a world in which it is real. The focus is on creating the context—the world—not the stories that inhabit it. The original "What if" proposition is the wellspring for engineering all aspects of the world including natural sciences, social structures, culture, technology, economics, health, and so on. The building covers the ecology of matter, the social ecology (dealing with human interactions), and the mental ecology (frames, ideas, beliefs, ideologies). It is a world guided by a speculative originating idea. World building provides an opportunity to change everything from chemistry to politics, from art to religion. It is an opportunity to start anew under different terms.

"World Building is founded on three beliefs, namely that storytelling is the most powerful system for the advancement of human capability due to its ability to allow the human imagination to precede the realization of thought; that all stories emerge logically and intuitively from the worlds that create them; and that new technologies powerfully enable us to sculpt the imagination into existence."
— The World Building Institute[91]

Worlds you build must be rich, intricated, coherent, and immersive. You can research world building methods and consult the World Building Institute's materials and videos for more.

KEY ELEMENTS OF WORLD BUILDING

Origin story: Sets in motion a chain of events that creates a causal framework and comes directly from the "What if" question.

Example: The movie *Minority Report:* What if there were a future in which capital crime no longer exists?

Logic points: Guides for design, assumptions that everyone buys into.

Setting is in Washington D.C., 2030; it is plausible.

If world building appeals to you, explore more at the World Building Institute at https://worldbuilding.institute.

EXPLORE WITH EMPATHY

Enchanted Brands only work if they connect, and to create that connection we must have empathy. Empathy is about being emotionally and cognitively embedded in a situation. It is about feeling, thinking, and perceiving things from an internal frame of mind rather than from an external objective one. More than just understanding something, empathy means we know how to identify with it. Empathy has three facets. First, having "empathetic concern" means we recognize and sense another's emotional state. Second, when we have "perspective taking" we are able to take another's perspective by imagining ourselves as the other person and moving toward a deeper understanding of their underlying feelings, thoughts, and value-based perspectives. This is the old "stand in another man's shoes" idea. Third, experiencing "emotional contagion" is where were we actually share the emotions, thoughts, and value-based perspectives of the other. These three build on each other to give us a deep, empathetic understanding.[92]

Brand Archeology Tools

I like to use specific tools in a process I call brand archeology. Here are my three favorite tools: the brand inventory, the brand snapshot, and the brand tapestry.

Brand Inventory

The brand inventory is a free-association exercise used to uncover the complete portfolio of words that someone has in their mind about the brand. Ask people in the focus group, "When I say Brand X, you think _____" and write down all their answers. I keep probing until they have nothing more to say. Then go back and ask the group to decide on the top five associations. Sometimes the inventory is deep, sometimes shallow. It's fascinating to see what makes up the brand.

Brand Snapshot

This exercise involves asking people to write down a visual picture of the brand. For robust brands, people often have a detailed picture in their mind. Budweiser, for example, may trigger a picture of young men relaxing at a bar after work, letting off steam. For Burger King, the visual picture might be rowdy teens in a restaurant that needs to be cleaned (I actually heard this). For some brands, people may have difficulty coming up with a visual picture. They might just see a logo or package.

Brand Tapestry

This exercise involves asking people to use a series of metaphorical images to tell the brand story. I provide a deck of images and ask the participants to choose images to explain the brand to me. They are to place the most important images in the center, with increasingly less important images in rings outside the center all the way out to the outer ring. Watch and listen as they create the brand tapestry. Was it difficult? Easy? What was the mood of the dialogue? Note the words and any issues. After allowing about twenty minutes, allow a group spokesperson to present the final piece, explaining the selection and placement of each photo. This is a great way to visualize how the brand exists. The point of this exercise is to encourage people to tap into their deep-seated ideas about the brand that come from a deeper consciousness. Therefore, it's important to select highly metaphorical images.

I have found brand tapestries to be one of the most powerful ways for people to explain the brand. For example, when I was working with Johnson & Johnson, the brand tapestry underscored how highly distinctive the company's brand was. The competitive brands, such as Merck and Bayer, chose central images of laboratory coats, beakers, dollar signs, and technology. For Johnson & Johnson, however, they chose pictures of loving mothers. If you were one of the world's top pharmaceutical companies, with products that might harm or kill people, which brand would you want?

TAKEAWAYS

- Rigorously understand and asses what is of value with your current brand as you don't want to leave hard-earned brand equity behind.
- Assess competitive brands relative to your brand, so you understand the way your target views the brands. They view brands in relation to one another, not isolated.
- Define what you want to keep, change, and lose as imperative to your process.
- Establish a brand trajectory that defines where your brand is today, where you want it to end up, and the Enchanted Brand identity that will get you there.

QUESTIONS TO EXPLORE

- What perceptions are of greatest value for your brand, which ones do you want to develop, and which ones do you want to lose?
- What does the future say about the kind of Enchanted Brand you want to create?

11
How to Create an Enchanted Brand Culture

"The most powerful and enduring brands
are built from the heart."
— **Howard Schultz**[93]

"There is a clear connection between a sense of purpose
that delivers positive impacts for all stakeholders and
sustained business success. Furthermore, leaders need
to articulate a culture of purpose–and, equally import-
ant, serve as a visible, consistent example of those be-
haviors. That's a terrific blueprint for any organization
that wants to become and remain exceptional."
— **Punit Renjen, CEO Deloitte**[94]

WELCOME BACK TO THE HUMAN SIDE OF BUSINESS—THE reason why Enchanted Brands are so important today. Now that we have the brand identity solution, it is time to move into action. This action begins at home, on the inside of the organization. This is not 1980s marketing where we now move into creating a multi-million-dollar advertising campaign to build the brand. It's not that easy. For an Enchanted Brand to ring true, it must be authentic within your company. The expectations created on the outside, must be met with delivery on the inside. If not, there will disappointment, dissonance, and failure. Building an Enchanted Brand culture is necessary, worthwhile, and trans-formative, and it starts with passionate, engaged leadership. In this chapter, I'll cover what leadership needs to do and provide guidelines on how to align, train, and activate the culture so it becomes a brand-building machine.

"It is a precarious time. This time one year ago, in January 2018, 132 CEOs left their posts, some of them under very difficult conditions, eight of them under transgressions. Ten left under difficult circumstances and 21 were replaced by their boards. That is the highest movement in CEOs that we have seen for eight years. This is not a time for your CEO to be sitting back. It is a time to be vocal, a time to be out there."
— **Kylie Wright-Ford, CEO of Reputation Institute**[95]

An Enchanted Brand is one of the CEO's most powerful tools, because the future belongs to those who can best manage the human side of business. For an Enchanted Brand to work its magic, the brand manager must be the CEO. Historically, powerful and enchanting brands have CEOs that love the brand, build it, protect it, help it shine and empower everyone to get behind it. They recognize and treat it as a priceless asset. From Jim Burke and Ralph Larsen at Johnson & Johnson to Sara Blakely of Spanx, to Steve Jobs of Apple, Andy Grove of Intel, and Richard Branson of Virgin.

Every powerful brand must have brand awareness (if no one knows your brand, you don't have one); perceived relevance (if it's not seen as relevant, it has no value to customers or the company); and trust (if customers don't believe you'll deliver what you promise, they won't buy your product). A powerful brand has all three and if one of them is missing, it doesn't matter how big the other two are. For example, trust has to be earned by keeping your promises and not letting people down. This means that the company needs to deliver on the brand which means people within the company must embrace it and own it—and this requires buy-in and leadership at the very top.

ENCHANTMENT STARTS AT THE TOP

They say the fish always stinks from the head. Likewise, enchantment starts at the top. Think Steve Jobs and Apple. People look for truth by observing the behavior of their leaders. In today's VUCA world, there seems to be a crisis in leadership. We observe industries in death spirals because they can't keep up with change; a diminishment of institutional vigor, and trust in global institutions; and the loss of dignity and output among displaced workers. More than ever, employees need to believe in their companies and to trust that those at the top are leading faithfully with the best interest of people, humanity and the planet in mind. Kawasaki proposes that the relationship between company culture and employee enchantment are one and the same. He says, "CEO" should stand for "Chief Enchantment Officer."[96] It's hard to imagine disenchanted employees enchanting customers and enchanted employees disenchanting customers. To meet the new challenges of human side of business, leaders need to embrace enchantment and build Enchanted Brand cultures. Much of it comes down to trust. Trust is built overtime on openness, humility, and honesty and is demonstrated beyond words. In fact, promising and not delivering is a sure way to erode trust.

"It is not advertising that produces great brand and reputation, it is trustworthiness, credibility and delivering against a brand promise. I think we have seen many stories in the last several years of what happens when CEOs don't safeguard their own brands or the brands of their corporations, or where corporations don't live up to the trust that is instilled in them or bestowed upon them by the marketplace and the constituencies and the stakeholders they are trying to serve."
— Cathy Bessant, Chief Operations and Technology Officer at Bank of America[97]

Culture change comes from concrete and noticeable changes in leadership behavior: what they do; who they hire; who they ask to move on; who they listen to and emulate; where they spend their time; what they talk about in meetings; what they measure; how they invest the firm's money. You need a leadership team that's committed to change, points the company in the right direction, sets the tone, establishes expectations, and leads by example.

I am not qualified to provide guidance on leadership, but others have done so in various ways across in many texts. My focus is only to help leaders understand how to make an Enchanted Brand succeed and why it requires leading like James Tiberius Kirk with the Starship Enterprise: leading people to "to boldly go where no man has gone before."

ENCHANTMENT TO MANAGE THE HUMAN SIDE OF BUSINESS

As discussed in chapter 4, our VUCA world has thrown humanity into a confusing, turbulent cyclone. Our human ability to adapt is being overtaken by the increasing pace of technolo-gy-driven change. It is getting harder for leaders to draw upon past experiences as a model for how to build the future. In this new era of business, every leader is going to have write to her or his own playbook for the future. There is no textbook to follow and there are new rules. Historically, CEOs focused on maximiz-ing shareholder value, often at the expense of employees, broader community (vendors, contractors, partners), and sometimes the planet. Now, CEOs need to put people before profits—and that is an enormous change. They need to rethink company culture and build a cultural fabric that brings out the best in everyone as individuals and as a group, so they may thrive during unthinkable change.

As mentioned in chapter 7 top-performing brands increase valuation and revenue growth, loyalty and rapid adoption of new products and ideas, mitigate risk, strengthen resilience, and reduce downside losses. They are growth drivers and risk reducers. What do Grey Goose and Accenture have in common? It is that brand equity accounts for a significant proportion of company value.

"If you look at the stock market during the last decade, intangible asset values were something like 60% of global valuations. In absolute terms the total value of intangibles is something like $55 trillion, and a large proportion of that is brand. And it's very clear from our analysis that strongly-branded companies outperform stock markets by up to 100%."
— Brand Finance CEO David Haigh[98]

Here, I will focus on the value of Enchanted Brands specifically for addressing the highly volatile human side of business-people in a VUCA world where there is low trust and high anxiety between people and institutions. Enchanted Brands are uniquely suited to use emotional and intellectual power to penetrate indifference, break through resistance, and inspire action. Rather than dictate or coerce, they open a pathway to trust and allow people to enter on their own volition. No Enchanted Brand can wield its magic without vigorous leadership by the CEO.

EVERYONE AND EVERYTHING SPEAKS FOR THE BRAND

Here is one immutable fact. If the CEO does not believe in the value of the brand, get excited about the brand and work to build the brand—no one else will.

To succeed, Enchanted Branding needs to be an enterprise-wide endeavor. Employees need to feel they own the Enchanted Brand, want to protect it, and work hard to build it. With an Enchanted Brand culture, employees will personify the brand and translate it directly to products, services, and company interactions. Think Disney. Think Virgin. Think the Four Seasons. Think REI. Strong brand cultures drive better business performance, attract and retain the best talent, and create a safe, positive work environment with less risk. Companies without strong brand cultures run the risk of their employees feeling disconnected and undervalued. Enchanted Brands become the fabric that brings the culture together and inspires people to be at their best.

Because Enchanted Brands are not built from traditional advertising and marketing but from a comprehensive range of corporate-wide activities delivered throughout the organization, there are implications for all company functions. Branding is a responsibility reaching far beyond the marketing and communications departments. Since the marketing does not have authority over other company functions, for example, frontline staff where actions can quickly cause the brand promise to deteriorate, they cannot implement necessary actions. They will only be able to influence the process with CEO authority behind them. Therefore, the CEO must take charge of the brand strategy, lead the brand development, oversee implementation, and be engaged in performance tracking if there is to be traction and success.

LEADERS GOTTA LEAD

Employees continually watch their leaders for cues about how to act. They are used to "initiative du jour" and often take a "wait and see" approach before they stop conserving energy and fully engage. More often than we'd like to admit, leaders say one thing and do another, which fosters a dispiriting process, with confusion and uncertainty eventually leading to lost motivation and trust. Ultimately, when resources are re-allocated to support brand activation, political interests often sideline initiatives unless the CEO steps in to make it clear that branding is a top priority. This is not as easy as it sounds.

According to the Deloitte's Core Beliefs and Culture survey, there is gap between what executives and employees believe when it comes to core values and beliefs. Of executives, 84% believe senior leadership communicates core values and beliefs, but only 67% of employees believe this correct. Similarly, 81% of execs believe the behavior of senior leadership complies with the core values and beliefs and only 69% of employees agree. Interestingly, employees equally value business strategy and core values and beliefs, while executives put business strategy well ahead. Most important, only 19% of executives and 15% of employees believed the company culture is in strong operation.[99] Finally, according to Gallup, 70% of American workers considered themselves disengaged during the first half of 2012.[100]

The CEO must work hard to fill these gaps and that means walking, talking, and living the Enchanted Brand. In addition, no brand reaches its goals unless the chairman and CEO buy in and back it up with the resources. This is why it is so important that senior leaders have a holistic and in-depth understanding of how branding works.

STRONG CULTURE MATTERS

Volumes have been written on the importance of having a strong culture in running a business. Stronger cultures drive better business performance, attract and retain the best talent, and create safe, positive work environments with less risk. Within every company, regardless of size or sector, culture unites to create a solid foundation for a lasting success. Building a vibrant culture allows employees to thrive and personify your brand in a positive way. The brand culture you create should translate directly to the products or services you offer, and how your company interacts with clients. Each piece should line up strategically and creatively to have the maximum impact.

Exceptional organizations have a two-sided ledger that not only strikes a balance between strategy and culture, but also connects them. Deloitte's survey, which polled approximately 300 executives and 1,000 employees from companies nationwide, found that 94 percent of executives and 88 percent of employees believe a distinct workplace culture is important to business success.[101] According to a recent survey by the National Bureau of Economic Research, 85 percent of CEOs and CFOs believe an unhealthy culture leads to unethical behavior. What's more, that same survey found that nine out of ten CFOs believe improving company culture would increase their company's business value and performance.[102]

CHAPTER 11

RECOVERING THE HUMAN SIDE OF BUSINESS

The human side of business has been in trouble for a long time as people have become increasingly marginalized by "maximizing shareholder value" and policies that put profits before people. It is now understood that this longstanding approach not only negatively impacts the internal organization, its leadership and employee engagement, but also affects customer experience, and partnerships. We must now figure out how to prioritize people over profits. Because, to realize profits, we must produce happy, trusted, and loyal staff, who want to succeed and, in turn, cause the company to succeed. It's that simple.

It always comes down to people.

When it comes to the execution of big-picture ideas and the Enchanted Brand, it comes down to how people work together, both within organizations and in partnerships between organizations. We can add all the technology in the world to a business, but it's still the people who drive the organization forward. Always, at some point, there is going to be resistance from a person who needs to be dealt with compassionately as a human, and not in a mechanical or rigid way. Whatever the extent of the change—disruption in the processes, product, structure, technology, people, and the organization—the adaptation is only successful if people are inspired and influenced for buy-in, commitment, acceptance, and adoption of the change.

Leaders may believe they're putting in the work to build and improve, but the reality is that employees don't agree according to Deloitte's Core Beliefs and Culture survey. Nearly half of employees (45 percent) say leadership is minimally or not at all committed to improving culture.[103] This discrepancy can lead to harrowing business repercussions, such as voluntary turnover that can cost organizations up to two times an employee's annual salary.

RE-HUMANIZING WORK

Part of strengthening the human side of business is to create a humanized workplace and community. The Enchanted Brand can be used to build this community and environment by providing the following enabling elements.

Belief: A person's words and actions will always follow their beliefs. Beliefs are connected to values and an Enchanted Brand gives life to values.

Empowerment: An Enchanted Brand is about empowerment and seeks to instill confidence and embolden people so they can see where their actions benefit themselves and others around them.

Structure: Enchanted Brands help people to embrace structures and systems for fewer mistakes and greater success, and they also foster exceptional human experiences.

Purpose: Everyone needs to connect their role and personal purpose within the company and the Enchanted Brand should make that connection.

Enchanted Brands can take the fear out of change and make it an adventure by activating the extraordinary human capacity to learn and adapt by engaging the imagination. Enchanted Brands are participatory and invite *active participation* in change. This requires a leadership shift: from seeing human beings as an instrument of change to seeing them as the authors and leaders of it. Sounds enchanting right? An Enchanted Brands gives people motivation, engenders commitment to change, and connects purpose and possibility by highlighting the following areas.

Personal Relevance: Helps people experience a deeper sense of purpose, so they are more awake and alive to their full potential.

Emotional Drivers: Evokes enabling emotions that inspire people to be their best selves.

Group Cohesion: Aligns people around shared motivations with a rallying spirit.

Sense of Belonging: Creates a strong emotional bond and sense of community.

Clarity: Symbolically communicates and represents vision, strategy, and expectations.

An Enchanted Brand culture can be the crucial difference between an organization becoming exceptional—or coming apart during metamorphosis. Unlike traditional brands, Enchanted Brands liberate hearts and minds by engaging the imagination and filling gaps to connect value and purpose, change and progress, challenge and opportunity and to reinforce individual value and relevance. That's a lot of heavy lifting. An Enchanted Brand is kind of like a magic wand, because as enchanting ideas are powerful. They are what launch revolutions. Give me liberty or give me death.

CREATING AN ENCHANTED BRAND CULTURE

In a world of transparency and authenticity, the brand inside and the brand outside must match. In other words, you cannot just create, produce, and disseminate an Enchanted Brand as a creative object. It must translate into a philosophy and set of core values that people can assimilate and express with their work. You'd be surprised at the number of companies that launch a new brand but fail to train their employees and get them on board.

The best part about building an Enchanted Brand culture is that it brings enchantment into the workplace. It delivers on three drivers of a strong culture:

1. Highlights that profit is not purpose. Profit is an outcome of purpose.
2. Defines an organization's higher calling well beyond maximizing the bottom-line.
3. Helps everyone understand how their work contributes.

When we translate the Enchanted Brand to the culture, it is important to have a cultural doctrine or short manifesto that connects purpose, possibility, individual responsibility, and collective accountability.

STEPS TO BUILDING AN ENCHANTED BRAND CULTURE

To create an employee culture of empowerment and engagement by linking purpose to role. Explore the following:

- Commit to culture and improving the human side of business as the top driver of business performance.
- Start by courageously facing your culture today—see it for what it really is, know the strengths and weaknesses, as well as systemic problems and opportunities.
- Be willing to invest in actions and tools to build the culture to align values and enable executives and employees to connect, relate, and act as one.
- Recognize this process takes time, requires sensitive monitoring, and needs continuous improvement
- Define the goals of building your Enchanted Brand culture. What do you aim to accomplish?

- Makes a list of the top five cultural changes that need to happen to become a strong culture.
- Define the challenges and obstacles to creating the change
- Invest in training sessions to align and activate employees around the Enchanted Brand doctrine and provide a toolkit they can use to build the culture.
- Invite employees to immerse in an enchanting experience and discuss it.
- Allow employees to form work teams, discussion forums, problem-solving studios, bootcamps, hackathons, and more to find diverse ways to come together and unleash their best thinking and imagination to solve the problems and implement solutions.

Brand Tool Example: Brand Value Matrix

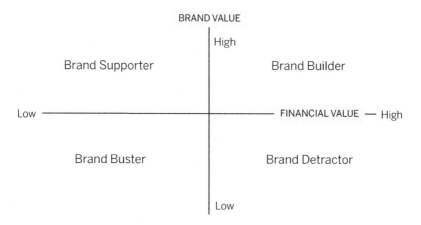

KEEP IT SIMPLE, WORK IT OVER TIME

When launching the new Enchanted Brand culture, start with small wins that are visible so people can see change. Seeing is believing. This could be as simple as changing signs and furniture. Engage employees to do the work. Pay them to roll up their sleeves and create change. Start with things that can easily be done and move to bigger challenges when there is enough runway for success. Sequence things properly.

RECOGNIZE EXCELLENCE, LET PEOPLE SHINE

Not everyone will want to become activated. Some will sit on the sideline and others will critique. That will not stop progress from happening. Embrace the skeptics and contrarians rather than silence or eliminate them. In time, most of them will come along or decide to leave. Reward those who do participate and make this work a pathway to leadership and growth. Have the CEO personally recognize outstanding efforts and contributions.

COMPANIES NEED TO PRACTICE ENCHANTMENT

Enchantment is idealistic and often surprising. The magic is in the doing. The best way to demonstrate enchantment is to make it happen and celebrate it when it does. Many years ago, Starbucks lost three employees during a robbery at one of its stores. Rather than send condolences from afar, its CEO flew cross-country to spend an entire week with employees and their families in the area. Enchanting. Some years later, a Starbucks barista offered one of her customers much more than a free refill. Knowing that her long-time customer desperately needed a kidney transplant and had no suitable donor, she took a blood test. A few days later, she told her astonished customer that she was a match. Whether it was culture, individual compassion, or both, the connection of values and actions sets an example for others to follow. That's enchanting.

"Enchant your customers, and then give your employees the freedom to enchant them, too. Your employees will come up with great ways that you've never considered. Let that happen; and then get out of your employees' way!"
— **Guy Kawasaki**[104]

Strong Brand Culture Example: Nike's Eleven Maxims

It is our nature to innovate.

1. Nike is a company.
2. Nike is a brand.
3. Simplify and go.
4. The consumer decides.
5. Be a sponge.
6. Evolve immediately.
7. Do the right thing.
8. Master the fundamentals.
9. We are on the offense—always.
10. Remember the man [the late Bill Bowerman, Nike co-founder].

Source: Nike, Inc.

TAKEAWAYS

- We must put people before profits and strengthen the human side of business.
- Enchanted Brands help to unleash the imagination and evoke the emotions needed to connect purpose and possibility, belief with values, actions with personal relevance.
- An Enchanted Brand requires a CEO who role-models commitment.
- Culture is critical to creating an engaged and high-performing workforce and community.
- Most companies do not have strong cultures and people feel disconnected and undervalued.
- Enchanted Brands can help by becoming the fabric that brings the culture together and inspires people to be at their best.
- Align, engage, and train everyone in Enchanted Branding so they can spread the enchantment which will increase value across your business.

QUESTIONS TO EXPLORE

- What is an honest description of your culture today?
- What are the challenges or obstacles to building a stronger culture?
- Is your leadership team capable of creating enchantment?

12
Enchanting Your Personal Professional Brand

WE LIVE IN A GIG ECONOMY WHERE MANY OF US MOVE frequently from assignment to assignment, working with different employers. Others are entrepreneurs or artists selling talents and building a public persona. We have become "talent" products in a vast talent marketplace and need to authentically differentiate, resonate and connect with those that matter. To succeed as with any competitive marketplace, you need to brand. To succeed in a VUCA world, you need to give yourself an Enchanted "Professional" Brand.

Your Enchanted Personal "Professional" Brand is part fact and part fiction in that it represents a packaged "you" that provides a deliberate lens through which you want to be seen. For example, you may be a stay-at-home suburban mom with a decade of financial services experience or a dynamic financial services manager with strong managerial and creative problem skills that enable great outcomes. Your Enchanted Brand assists in defining who you are, what makes you great, and why you should be hired. It not only communicates your reputation and value to an employer, but also the secret sauce of you.

WELCOME TO THE GIG ECONOMY

The term "gig" is slang for a job that lasts a specified period of time and was coined by musicians. It has grown to become a core component of the labor market, causing companies to review their definitions of what it means to be an employee. Organizations are starting to find some of their best talent through gig labor arrangements. Roughly 57 million Americans (37 percent of American workers) are gig workers, according to *Forbes*.[105] Nearly one in four Americans earn money from the digital "platform economy," according to the Pew Research Center.[106]

The gig economy is a labor market characterized by the prevalence of short-term contracts or freelance work. It is a free market system in which temporary positions are common and organizations hire independent workers for short-term commitments. Gig employees can include freelancers, independent contractors, project-based workers, and temporary or part-time hires. As of 2021, 36 percent of the U.S. work force is in the gig economy, an estimated 59 million people.[107] This is also known as the "alternative workforce." Businesses save resources in terms of benefits, office space, and training and have the ability to contract with experts for specific projects who might be too high-priced to maintain on staff. There are many websites now for gig recruiting including Behance.net for creative work or Toptal for information technology.

There are several forces behind the rise of the gig economy, including digital technologies that allow workers to be mobile and work from anywhere; financial pressures on businesses leading to the creation of a more flexible workforce; and the entrance of the millennial generation, which is demanding a work-life balance that favors flexibility.[108] The gig economy is one of several new operating models transforming society along with the sharing economy (collaborative consumption, peer-to-peer based sharing), the gift economy (no payment for goods and services), and the barter economy (cashless economic system).

WHO IS IN THE GIG ECONOMY?

The gig economy covers a broad range of workers—skilled and unskilled, high-earning and low-earning—that have historically been referred to as contingent workers. According to the *Harvard Business Review,* these are "workers with specialized skills, deep expertise, or in-demand experience" and also, low-skill, low-wage workers in retail and service positions.[109] Many gig economy workers are Generation Xers who were laid off during the Great Recession and turned to gig work. According to the Aspen Institute, between 2010 and 2014 nearly 30 percent of jobs created were independent contract positions.[110]

A Staffing Industry Analysts (SIA) study, conducted before the COVID-19 pandemic, estimates that 44 million Americans who have taken part in the gig economy fall into the following categories:

- Independent contractors or self-employed workers: 23.5 million.
- Human cloud workers: 9.7 million.
- Temporary workers assigned through a staffing agency: 9.5 million.
- Temporary employees sourced directly: 5.5 million.
- Statement-of-work consultants employed by a consulting firm: 2.9 million.[111]

An Aspen Institute survey of gig economy workers says the highest concentrations of U.S. gig economy workers reside in the Pacific and Mountain regions, with the lowest concentration in the upper Midwest and New England. They are more likely than the average worker to work from home and nearly 60 percent of all gig workers are male with a median age of fifty years old.[112]

COMPETING IN THE GIG ECONOMY

The gig marketplace is comprised of millions of people and it's easy to be lost at sea, especially in world where "contactless" hiring is now common. Your professional Enchanted Brand will help you to break through and shine. Like any powerful brand, it will highlight your strengths, establish a reputation, build trust, and communicate unique attributes. It will attract the right people and communicate that you are the right fit. An overwhelming 85 percent of hiring managers report that a candidate's professional brand influences their hiring decisions.[113]

In pragmatic terms, a professional brand is what matters to a potential employer or anyone who can help you find a job or grow your career. You want to take control of your professional brand and shape it. If you don't, other forces may do it for you.

CREATING YOUR PERSONAL
PROFESSIONAL ENCHANTED BRAND

Your professional brand will need a clear focus that resonates with your target audience and is true to your essence. Just as with developing any Enchanted Brand, start with a discovery process that provides insights into building the strategic foundation for creating the identity you wish to convey. When it comes time to express your Enchanted Brand, you may even craft a tagline that enchants. Apple challenged the world to "Think Different," Nike encouraged people to "Just Do It," and Dunkin' Donuts told busy professionals that "America Runs on Dunkin.'" These slogans have told a story and influenced how people perceive the organizations behind them. What will yours say about you?

In your discovery process, work to create a clear picture of the industry you are targeting, the people you want to reach, and what peers and competitors are saying. Also, it helps to do a little primary research to further uncover the skills and traits that make you distinct. I know it may be awkward, but talk to peers, colleagues, friends and family who have worked with you to hear what they have to say.

- What are three words that you would use to describe the best parts of me?
- What kind of work culture best fits me?
- What makes me special?
- How would you characterize who I am and what I bring?

Once you have a list your list of words that describe you, put them into a free word-cloud generator, such as Wordle, as that visual may help you. The biggest words are the ones used most often to describe you.

SET YOUR BRAND TRAJECTORY

Using the tools from chapter 9, create a brand trajectory for your personal and professional Enchanted Brand.

Brand Position: Get to know your personal professional brand as it exists today. Ask professional peers and co-workers to describe your strengths, passions, accomplishments, uniqueness and profile. Google yourself. What do you find? This is your current "brand position."

Brand Ideal: Now, think about what you want your brand to be in the future—in an ideal world. This is the brand ideal discussed in chapter 9. Be vivid in your description and include characteristics, skills, and attributes, such as "great leader" and "rare innovator." Vision and imagine. Do not be shy. Dream. You can collaborate with friends and family and look for examples. Maybe you like the vision of Bill Gates, the passion of Steve Jobs, the pragmatic smarts of Warren Buffet, the courage of Mike Tyson, the coolness of Kanye West, or the poise of Michelle Obama. Explore diverse people. Also, think about what you want to be known for. Now, draw your professional brand trajectory, brand position to brand ideal.

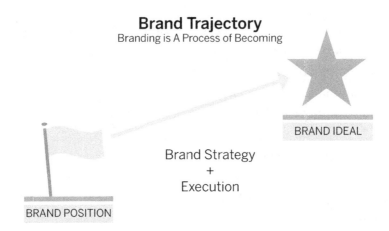

Brand Trajectory
Branding is A Process of Becoming

BRAND IDEAL

Brand Strategy
+
Execution

BRAND POSITION

Now you know where you are, and ideally where you want to end up with your brand. Next, create the Enchanted Brand Identity that will move your brand toward its ideal state.

DEFINE YOUR BRAND AUDIENCE

Know you are reaching several communities with your brand and probably crossing several industries. Identify the individuals that matter, such as thought leaders and influencers, and the companies that will hire you, such as recruiters and leadership executives. Create pictures of the people. Get to know them as people. Understand their challenges and dreams. Figure out what all of these people have in common. What unites them? Are they visionary thinkers changing the world? Are they passionate experts facing new challenges?

SELF-DIRECTIONING

To clarify your intentions and value, work through the following areas:

1. Vision: In one sentence, describe the professional world you are in and why you are needed.
2. Opportunities and challenges: What are the challenges and barriers you face as well as the opportunities?
3. Value Proposition: What value and what unique value do you create?
4. Credibility: What enables you to create this value? Talents, skills, expertise, experience, assets, education, cultural background? What enables you to deliver your unique value?
5. Definition: How would you label what you do? For instance— plumber, architect, lawyer, or sculptor?
6. Values: What are the three to five values that govern how you work?
7. Ideal Work Environment: What kind of company or situation do you most want to work with? What kind of company do you *not* want to work with? Describe vividly.
8. Dream Experience: What kind of work experience do you want? Describe vividly.
9. Brand Objective: What do you want your brand to do for you?

Ultimately, you are going to create a "brand statement" that reflects your goals, secret sauce, and enchantment. Here's a guide to unleash your imagination and help you sculpt the poetic professional you.

ENCHANTED BRAND PERSONAL PROFESSIONAL BLUEPRINT

1. ***Mission:*** Define your mission as your intentions. I intend to create X value for Y kind of organizations by providing Z kind of contribution.

2. ***Positioning:*** Think of this as framing or reframing you beyond the literal job description. Are you a branding guru? Chief Confusion Officer? Visionary Technology Pioneer? For inspiration, explore LinkedIn and Twitter and see what others have done.

3. ***Promise:*** State succinctly what you can do for the person who may work with you. This should be both rational and emotional. Perhaps you can drive sales and create a happy, fulfilled sales team. Maybe you can make customers happy and unearth ideas for improving efficiencies. Your unique value stems from who you are as a person and what you do.

4. ***Brand Personality:*** The greatest challenge for employers is finding the right cultural fit. People want to know the kind of personality they are hiring. Make this authentic as you also want a good fit. Are you a cool, hip, trend-setting tastemaker? Are you a hard-charging, results-driven, game-changer? Are you a quiet leader? Conceptualize your personality. Sherlock Holmes? James Bond? Jack Welsh meets Jamie Dimon?

5. ***Brand Values:*** Describe the value that you hold dear and want to be honored by others.

6. ***Brand Credibility:*** Articulate the most important things that makes your unique value credible. This isn't your resume. It doesn't always have to involve your educational background or job history. It could also be passion or vision.

7. ***Brand Purpose:*** In a sentence, describe what drives you? What is your higher calling? What is the impact you hope to

have in the world? This adds depth to your identity. How do you want to make the world a better place?

8. ***Enchanted Brand Idea:*** What idea or metaphor captures you? Are you a diamond in the rough? A David that can slay Goliaths? A mad genius who can save the world? Are you a romantic bringing beauty to design? Find a colorful, accurate, enchanting way to capture your essence. Maybe it is in a song title, a play, or a piece of poetry? Are you the prodigal son? The road less travelled? The underdog? A late bloomer with blooming potential? This idea or metaphor will show more of your essence.

CREATE YOUR ENCHANTED BRAND IDENTITY

Brand Identity Statement: Write a one- or two-sentence phrase that accurately sums up what you do and what you stand for. It's your unique selling proposition, the thing you do best. Make it enchanting. The best statements are catchy, memorable, and attention-grabbing. It needs to be short while also conveying the value you provide to employers, clients, or customers. It should also have a certain level of intrigue that makes people want to learn more about you. For example:

"I help thought leaders write great books in just ninety days. Three hundred satisfied clients so far."

Portrait Photo: Like a good actor, get a great head shot of yourself. In many ways, this is your logo. I recommend doing what actors do: find a local head shot photographer as they know how to create career-building head shots, and they are also affordable. LinkedIn profiles with professional headshots receive roughly fourteen times more profile views and are thirty-six times more likely to receive a message.[114]

Personal Positioning Statement: Start using the positioning statement you created in your blueprint as a label on social media and wherever you identify yourself professionally.

E-mail Signature: We all use e-mail quite a bit. Use that opportunity to convey your brand with an e-mail signature that speaks. You can include your photo, links to your social media accounts, and even a phrase that highlights a recent accomplishment, for instance, "TED Speaker 2021" or "Featured in *Wired's* Top 1000 Entrepreneurs."

LinkedIn: For some, having a presence on Instagram, YouTube, Twitter, or even Spotify might be the ticket. It depends on where your audience is, and where you need to build a profile. Ninety-two percent of recruiters leverage social media to find high-quality candidates, so you want your brand to shine there. Be sure to focus on the platform that matters most. Do not be daunted. Most platforms have tools that make it easy. Regardless, put your brand on LinkedIn. It is the hotspot for executive recruiters and the "yellow pages" of talent.[115]

Leverage Your Network: Eighty-five percent of all jobs are filled through networking[116] so be sure to build your brand with friends and family, peers and industry thought leaders, online and in person. The more connections you make, the faster you will build your brand. Use the website Jibber Jobber to keep track of networking contacts and keep a log of how they have helped you.

Publish: Write a blog. Again, do not be daunted. Even if you write once a quarter, it is valuable. Share your thinking, flex your enchanted brain. A blog is a credential, an accomplishment. Post it on social networks and on your website and build a subscriber list who receive it via e-mail. Also, guest blogging is a great way to expand your audience and build credibility. Use social media, search engines, and search tools to identify the top websites in your niche. Create a list of potential websites where you can post as a guest. Next, see if they have a procedure for submitting ideas for articles. Some of the sites will have pages titled "Write for Us" or "Contribute." If you don't like to write, you can easily hire a ghost writer to do it for you.

Create an Active Presence Online: If you have time, comment on other people's blogs. Send them an e-mail or a message via their website or networking profile. Over the years, I've met lots of the important people in the world of job searching and careers, many of them because I sent them a quick e-mail introducing myself or vice versa.

Make a Video or Webinar: You can create an introductory video or a series of short videos where you show yourself in action. Consider creating a webinar—maybe you talk over twelve to twenty slides—that again shows you in action.

Don't just stay on the internet. You also need to be a real person in the real world building your brand.

Volunteer: If you have time and if there's a way to volunteer in a capacity where you can use your skills and expertise, volunteering is another way to gain exposure as an expert in your career field. Especially volunteer to be on a board, so you can add governance experience to your credentials.

Speak: The more people that see and hear you, the better. If you are shy and this is not your thing, skip it. No need to stress. This is only for some people and may not be necessary for what you do. However, if it is, try small civic, local professional organizations, conferences, and communities.

TAKEAWAYS

- Creating a professional brand is essential in the new gig economy.
- Building a professional brand just takes courage and commitment.
- Your professional brand must be authentic and also intriguing.
- Many of the processes and tools we use for enchanted product brands apply here.
- You must first figure out what your current brand is. Google yourself.
- Putting yourself out there

QUESTIONS TO EXPLORE

- What is holding me back from creating my professional brand?
- How do I overcome these barriers to the future I want to create?
- Who are the people I can call upon to help me?
- What is a comfortable timeframe for getting this done?
- What can I put in place that will prompt me forward if I slow down, get stuck, or give up?

13
Branding in a
Networked World

THIS EYE-OPENING AND POTENTIALLY MIND-BLOWING CHAPter is about how to create change in the hyperconnected, interdependent, real-time world. In this new world you create change by shaping it. You catalyze change rather than engineer it, and this process involves constant iteration, creativity, and elasticity. This chapter provides essential knowledge for anyone launching a new brand or rebranding. I hope it will help you come to grips with the new realities of a networked society and why traditional brand building methods no longer work.

While there are countless texts on modern marketing, this chapter focuses on a theory of change in our new world. Once you know this, you will start to see the world in a new way. I will discuss the importance of driving concepts such as resonance, emergence, and transmedia. In this chapter, I introduce the Enchanted Brand building model, which outlines the role of narratives, mechanisms of connection, and the networks that carry it all to put the brand into minds and into the culture.

Change is not driven by plans that are implemented, but by engaging deeply with the whole context (interrelated conditions of the environment) and shaping it while it is changing in often unpredictable and novel ways. If we look at the world as a series of continually emerging exchanges, we see the present as determined by the past, but its relationship to the future is one of influence and probability, not determinacy. We look at the past to understand the present, and we look at the present to understand the conditions that set up rather than determine the future.

BRANDING UNDER A NEW PARADIGM OF CHANGE

Once you have designed your Enchanted Brand identity, you need bring it to life and launch it into the world. Now, rather than dive into well-trodden paths on how to create brands through powerful communications, advertising, public relations, content, digital content, and so on, I'm going to bring you to a different place. There are countless texts and views on how to do modern marketing, but they do not take into account a fundamental shift in how change occurs today. I want you to focus on how change actually occurs in our new world. Once you know that, the lights will go on. You'll start to think about things in a new way, particularly how to translate your brand and how to move your brand into the world and have it consumed, used, and built by others.

Human beings have always been diversely motivated; we act for material gain, but also for psychological well-being and gratification; for social connectedness as well as power; for meaning capital as well as monetary/power capital. Embedded in networks, motivations lead to agency when we understand that normal cause and affect have limited meaning. Instead it is all flows and exchanges. These flows and exchanges cannot be dictated or planned, but they can be influenced.
—Anne Pendleton-Jullian and John Seely Brown, Design Unbound1[17]

Just as there was a paradigm shift from the industrial age to the digital age, there has been a shift in the forces, factors, and influences driving the evolution of society, politics, and human values. Methods of communication and networks of connectivity are both affecting and following this shift. While the industrial era was about control, and communications systems reflected that, our hyperconnected era is about community and networks reflect that shift. We see how our lives connect with others and how other worlds influence our own. Street-level communications, sharing, mobilization, and action have gained unprecedented power.

INFLUENCING IN A HYPERCONNECTED WORLD

We live in a VUCA world and accept that the future is unstable and unknowable. Making progress and shaping change requires an interchange between social, material, and technical elements. Everything is interconnected—and in motion. Since everything is changing all the time, it means Enchanted Brands must be catalytic rather than prescriptive. Unlike traditional brands, Enchanted Brands work to nudge forces already in play and do not attempt to control change—only to influence it.

In our adolescent networked society, hyperconnectivity has great promise and peril. Enabled by technology, this hyperconnectivity creates various social networks due to an expanded web of influential relationships that allow a person to experience greater meaning and power than ever before. In this new world, power is both concentrated (technocrats, tech platforms) and distributed (everyone has some) as more people are participating in ensembles of relationships woven together by different kinds of networks. Brands flow through these networks and these networks affect equity; so awareness of these networks and how they operate is critical to building your Enchanted Brand.

Consider how a person's relationships have expanded and how far participation reaches.

Personal: Personal relationships are closer with digital hyperconnectivity. Real-time, real-vivid connections via voice, text, video from any place to any place create greater participation and bonding.

Extra-personal: Personal networks are broadened through networks of interests, work and other trusted relationships, such as, my brother's friends.

Societal: People enjoy greater participation in larger societal structures, such as forums and communities.

Global: People now connect across multiple cultural settings.

The flow of intangibles, such as emotions, stories, knowledge, meaning, and brands through these networks is what builds identity and trust. Since decision-making power and the capacity to create influence flows through these networks, brands need to work within them. For brands to scale on impact and momentum, they need to ride across networks and also to act as a network.

NEW DYNAMICS OF THIS WORLD

These are some big ideas to understand about how this new way of catalyzing change is going to work.

Emergence: Refers to the process of something coming into existence. In the networked world, this is where simple interactions among individual parts or agents form complex behaviors and patterns at the systems level. Think about snowflakes, cities, the human immune system, and the global economy. Emergence is all around us.

Transmedia: First used in the 1990s by University of Southern California film scholar Marsha Kinder,[118] this term represents a process where integral elements of a fiction get dispersed systematically across multiple delivery channels for the purpose of creating a unified and coordinated entertainment experience—for instance, movies, books, video games, memes, tours, websites, and comics. Each platform delivers something new according to its genre and creates additional comprehension within a narrative system. Transmedia experiences draw people in and scale emotional participation and amplify content. The narrative space grows and the brand is enriched by contributions from others. You should explore using transmedia to distribute your Enchanted Brand.

Participation: This is not the passive world of the media gross rating point (GRP) where brands were transmitted via millions of advertising impressions to unwitting victims. Today, people want to participate and co-create with brands. The explosive phenomenon known as fan fiction is one example. This is where fans create unauthorized versions or expansions of the original content, often creating new stories and characters. User-generated brand content is another.

With the above in mind, let's set out to explore how to bring your Enchanted Brand to life. Warning: this path is based on the premise that we live in a VUCA world that is always in motion, fraught with emergence, and where the future can only be influenced rather than controlled.

THE ENCHANTED BRAND BUILDING MODEL

Enchanted Brands are built to shape change. Change must travel across the social networks by getting people to participate in the brand. There are five interrelated components that work individually and together to build the brand and influence change. Rather than using a brand, I will use the movie *Dead Poets Society* as a reference example to clarify understanding, as it provides an excellent illustration of the concept.[119]

1. Brand Change Purpose and Vision

This creates the motivational context for the brand and orients the ideas and elements of the branding efforts. It is strategic and big picture-oriented and frames everything. It is rarely communicated. It is more of a strategic rudder. In *Dead Poets Society,* Keating's vision was to empower each student to think for himself in an educational environment that was designed to mold students to follow prescribed pathways defined by their social class and demanded by their families.

2. Master Brand Narrative

This is the articulation and expressions of the big idea and brand supporting concepts translated into an orchestra of powerful branding agents (touchpoints)—think transmedia—that each capture and contribute an element of the brand. The master brand narrative operationalizes the vision and delivers on it. In *Dead Poets Society,* Keating did not tell students to break away, fight the system they were born into, and become their own unique personalities despite what teachers and families have planned. He had a big idea articulated in a rallying cry, *"Carpe diem"*—Seize the day. Make your lives extraordinary. He did not propose change.

He created a catalyst for change that appealed to their imaginations, sense of adventure, and desire to be unique. He created an Enchanted Brand.

Enchanted Brands demand engagement. They appeal to emotions and intellect. They look forward, are action-oriented, demand personal ownership and action. An Enchanted Brand feels like it is addressed uniquely to you, although it is universal. Like great art, different individuals will identify with it, and all are unified in the process of identifying with it. Enchanted Brands unify diversity with a common, compelling idea.

- The Army—Be All That You Can Be.
- John Templeton Foundation—Stay Curious.
- LMI—The Time to Make a Difference Has Never Been Greater.
- Club Med—The Antidote to Civilization.
- Ireland—The Ancient Birthplace of Good Times.

Like *Carpe Diem,* these create an open story, so that people can imagine what it would mean for them and assimilate the brand into their own world.

The master brand narrative must be provocative enough to incite action and lead to the building of a personal narrative (see below). It uses emotion to engage others to envision their individual role in the action of identifying themselves within it. Ideally, you want to achieve intrinsic commitment—a coupling of emotion to intellect and belief with purpose.

The master narrative reframes and, in doing so, can create transactional shifts. The master brand narrative comes to life across many levels—some less active than others such as a tagline, logo, website, and content. The master brand narrative is the engine of the Enchanted Brand. It creates a shared consciousness.

3. The Personal Brand Narrative

This is where the Enchanted Brand lives among the people. As individuals absorb the brand into their own narrative, they each create a personal brand narrative. It is their personal interpretation and assimilation. In doing so, they are now bonded to others who have done the same; yet everyone's personal narrative is unique. These narratives emerge from real experiences that help build identity. In *Dead Poets Society,* the boys actually form a club called the Dead Poets Society and that club gives each kid a personal "brand" experience. The way that people interpret these experiences is in relationship to how they sense their place in the world; how they understand, express, and affirm that place.

Personal narratives reveal how people define themselves through past events and the imagination and vision of their future. In this, they contain the seeds of change. These narratives are thin slices of interpretations that orbit around the same flow of information and express recurring themes. In *Dead Poets Society,* we see the stories of seven students who form the club. We see each of their unique backstories. As the film progresses, we see each in personal transformation, as well as the collective group transformation, as each person takes ownership of Keating's master brand idea and acts on it differently. At the same time, the group coalesces around the master brand narrative.

As mentioned at the start of our journey, the brand always belongs to the people. It lives out in the world in the imaginations of people. This personal narrative process of assimilation is how Enchanted Brands create the perceptions and perspectives that generate action. People share these experiences and associate emotions with others in their networks to find a common connection and, in doing so, build a larger sense of self. This builds the brand and creates actions. That is why we view the personal narrative as the gasoline fueling the engine.

4. Brand Mechanisms of Connection

Brand mechanisms do the work of *delivering* the brand, forging connection to brand, enabling deeper experiences with and participation in the brand, and enabling brand advocacy. While mechanisms are not content, they supply content and help the content to do the work it needs to do. Brand mechanisms can:

- Act as catalysts to initiate change
- Move content and information around
- Help passionate brand advocates come together and communicate
- Entice and propel brand advocates

In *Dead Poets Society,* poetry was the mechanism that gave the students a new way of relating to the world around them. It opened them up intellectually and emotionally to see the world through the eyes of the poets and it challenged them to act on their own instincts. The poetry provided emotional guidance to feelings they could not understand, let alone articulate. A second mechanism was the creation of the poetry society, the community that supported the risk-taking and became the safe place for reflection as their experiences unfolded.

Media, traditional or multi-modal, is a brand mechanism. It engages participants and circulates information in ways that engage the emotions and the mind. It can capture emotional attention better than any other mechanism. Think about the power of transmedia. Mechanisms can involve several layers of dissimilar activities that are communication- and media-based.

5. Branding Networks

The master brand narrative puts the idea in motion by creating a common platform. The personal narratives contribute to it, draw from it, and share it. The mechanisms take it and embed it in things designed to create change. However, the social networks are the ones that distribute the narratives and spread the work through the system. Social networks connect people, organizations, resources, and efforts. They provide the means and the transmission medium for content that is tangible (goods and services) and intangible (ideas, knowledge, information, intentions). It is through the flow of the intangibles that people build identity, trust, power, and social capital. These define who we are, influence what we believe, and think and shape our actions.

First, we must identify and understand the relevant network or networks. We need to be aware of flow direction and velocity. In *Dead Poets Society*, the communication path that does the transformation is singular and mostly flows in one direction. It is a challenge from Keating to his students that flows from Keating down to the students, consistently and passionately.

Second, networks are heterogenous and some people or groups of people are more influential. Working with these super-connectors accelerates the building of the brand and its influence.

Third, social networks are always reconfiguring themselves. They are relational, not transactional, and they can be reconfigured by introducing new narratives and communication methods into the system.

In building the Enchanted Brand, we must understand a given context, design the change we want to shape and create the narratives, mechanisms that drive the work of the system and understand the form and flow of existing networks. Remember, we are not starting from scratch. We are shaping what is.

This is a living process of watching, listening, learning, and recalibrating. As master brand narratives, personal narratives, and brand mechanisms flow, they create a wake of influence behind them. In the past, leadership greatly influenced personal narratives. Today, people construct their own narratives in a rich social network. We are catalyzing change, not engineering it. It is not a linear process. It is an engagement process of constant iteration, creativity, and elasticity.

WELCOME TO THE WORLD
OF BRAND ECOLOGY

Ecology theory helps us to understand that all components of a complex, evolving environment are constituent parts of an ecosystem. Let's go further on our far-out brand journey to explore how ecology theory suggests a systemic approach to understanding, building, and even leveraging brands. We will explore the use of brand ecosystems to thrive better in a networked society. The branding ecosystem concept is partially in response to an exponentially growing e-commerce universe producing seemingly infinite choices. Enchanted Brands can be aggregators and curators in this world that help simplify choice and increase connection. Whether or not you build a brand ecosystem, be aware that your brand exists within one, perhaps several ecosystems. It does not operate in a vacuum and is shaped by peer, competitive, complementary, and extension brands. Recognizing the interconnectedness of your brand will probably reveal risks, opportunities, and potentially new ideas for growth.

BRANDS AFFECT OTHER BRANDS

Although brands have traditionally been built with high walls and moats to compete against one another and win, all branding efforts work together creating a collective impact on people, society, and culture. Often, one brand affects others in the system.

When one pharmaceutical brand acts greedily and inappropriately, it can cast a shadow in all pharma brands. When a start-up tech firm shines, it can create a halo on similar brands. Brand ecosystem thinking builds on concepts of business ecosystems and ecology science. It is not new. It is also inspired by the work of Harvard evolutionary biologist Martin Nowak, who turned Darwin's "survival of the fittest" theory on its head by demonstrating that evolution was actually driven by cooperation. Those who cooperated, survived. Brands that act together in our new world, may find it easier to succeed.

ABOUT ECOSYSTEMS

In the 1930s, British botanist Arthur Tansley introduced the term "ecosystem" to describe a community of organisms interacting with each other and their environments—air, water, earth, and so on. In order to thrive, these organisms competed and collaborated with each other on available resources, co-evolved, and jointly adapted to external disruptions.[121]

Business strategist James Moore adopted this biological concept in his 1993 *Harvard Business Review* article, "Predators and Prey: A New Ecology of Competition," in which he made a parallel between companies operating in the increasingly interconnected world of commerce and a community of organisms adapting and evolving to survive.[122] Moore suggested that a company be viewed not as a single firm in an industry, but as a member of a business ecosystem with participants spanning across multiple industries.

Advances in technology and increasing globalization have changed ideas about the best ways to do business, and the idea of a business ecosystem is thought to help companies understand how to thrive in a rapidly changing environment. Moore defined the business ecosystem as follows:

An economic community supported by a foundation of interacting organizations and individuals—the organisms of the business world. The economic community produces goods and services of value to customers, who are themselves members of the ecosystem. The member organisms also include suppliers, lead producers, competitors, and other stakeholders. Over time, they co-evolve their capabilities and roles and tend to align themselves with the directions set by one or more central companies. Those companies holding leadership roles may change over time, but the function of ecosystem leader is valued by the community because it enables members to move toward shared visions to align their investments and to find mutually supportive roles.[123]

In effect, the business ecosystem consists of a network of interlinked companies that interact with each other dynamically through competition and cooperation in order to grow sales and survive. When an ecosystem thrives, it means that the participants have developed patterns of behavior that streamline the flow of ideas, talent, and capital throughout the system.

"In annual reports, the term ecosystem occurs 13 times more frequently now than it did a decade ago. This is a substantive new phenomenon: the rise of dynamic, multicompany systems as a new way of organizing economic activity. Seven of the world's 10 largest companies, all using technology to disrupt not only their sectors but broad swaths of the economy, now depend on such systems, and ecosystems thinking is more prominent in faster-growing companies across the S&P 500. The growing interest is driven by necessity: Business environments are evolving more rapidly, requiring the rapid acquisition and coordination of diverse, novel capabilities. The rise of ecosystems requires a new way of thinking about business— the ecosystems perspective."
— MIT Sloan Management Review, 2019[124]

Like business ecosystems, brand ecosystems are multi-entity, made up of brands not belonging to a single organization. They involve networks of shifting, semi-permanent brand relationships, linked by consumers, experiences, services, values, and, often, ideas. The relationships combine aspects of competition and collaboration, often involving complementarity between different products and capabilities (for instance, smartphone brands and app brands). Ecosystem players co-evolve as they redefine their capabilities and relations to others over time.

WHAT IS A BRAND ECOSYSTEM?

A brand ecosystem is a dynamic group of independent brands that create products or services that together constitute a coherent solution or idea. Each ecosystem is anchored by a concept and set of values, and by a clearly-defined, albeit changing, group of brands with different roles. A brand ecosystem can include marketplaces that bring together large numbers of producers of products or services and potential customers. For example, in e-commerce (Amazon, Venmo, FedEx), hospitality (Airbnb, TripAdvisor, Open Table), luxury travel (NetJets, Hinckley, Four Seasons), and fitness (Peloton, Lululemon, Equinox). Offerings can integrate components from different players, for example, video games, smart home systems, self-driving vehicles, home care, luxury vacations, and disease management platforms.

Brand ecosystems are indivisible and an environment where all brand associations affect the current and future perceptions of the system. The work of the brands in the ecosystem may be interconnected, but the brands are independent. The complex series of brand exchanges adapts to emerging trends, information, and practices, keeping the brand ecosystem relevant as the individual brands stay relevant.

There can be enormous diversity in brand ecosystems, but several characteristics are universal:

- *Cohesion:* rands are from independent companies yet function as part of an integrated whole. Customers can choose among component brands and combine brands in any way they want. Think of smartphone and apps brands—some are pre-installed, but most are selected by the user and downloaded from an app store.
- *Common Core:* Perceptions from brand ecosystem participants tend to adhere to the overall ecosystem structure and are mutually compatible. For example, all Whole Foods brands have "clean food and product" values such as non-GMO ingredients and minimally processing, while many are organic.

- *Coordination:* Brand ecosystems are not hierarchically controlled, but there tends to be some mechanism of coordination—for example, through standards and values.

The branding ecosystem concept is in response to an exponentially growing e-commerce universe and helps make decision making easier by breaking that universe into galaxies and worlds. In a global, online marketplace with seemingly infinite choice, they act as aggregators and curators. If hotels are part of the Hyatt hospitality system, they are imbued with certain characteristics and expectations. Players in a brand ecosystem align on characteristics such as quality and values, and each validates other component players. If you like GOOP, you'll be very open to trying brands that GOOP includes in its ecosystem and the same goes with Orvis, BMW, Fender, and Jeep. There is an expectation that is created and met by participating brands.

Brand ecosystems can be built around an activity, such as shaving, bathing, creating music, or around an idea such as slow cooking, family chi, high performance, or a standard such as green, quiet, sustainable, or even a feeling such as happy, enlightened, driven, or sexy.

There are three basic kinds of brand ecosystems, and possibly more:

1. Gatekeeper: Whole Foods, Apple
2. Curator: GOOP, Oprah
3. Lifestyle: Orvis, Jeep

Brand ecosystems create value for a company, consumers, and society by organizing energy around important concepts and values, efficiently sharing resources to better communicate those concepts and ideas and by simplifying the buying process. Like business ecosystems, brand ecosystems can create strong barriers to entry for new competition, as potential entrants have to compete against the entire system of independent complementing brands that form the network. Being a part of a brand ecosystem provides mechanisms to leverage shared technology, achieve excellence in and rapid innovation, drive efficiencies in sales and marketing, and compete more effectively against other companies.

Brand ecosystems also help to:

- Drive novel collaborations to address emerging challenges.
- Increase creativity and innovation by focusing on fundamental and emerging human needs, desires, and dreams.
- Accelerate learning by collaborating, sharing insights, skills, expertise, and knowledge.

When you reflect your brand, you should consider building a brand ecosystem if:

- You face an unpredictable but highly malleable business environment that requires collaboration with others in order to shape or reshape the industry.
- The individual components of the consumer solution can be easily and flexibly combined to create a new benefit.
- An ecosystem improve access to capabilities, markets, and fast scaling.

TAKEAWAYS

- In a VUCA world you cannot engineer change, only shape it.
- People operate within vast social networks which largely influence trust and choice.
- Enchanted Brands are catalysts that must travel across systems and leverage certain narratives and mechanisms to be effective.
- Although brands are unique, they are interdependent with other brands.
- Brands need to leverage cooperation over competition to excel and contribute to the world.
- Brand ecosystems create time and cost efficiencies to benefit all parts of the human side of business.

QUESTIONS TO EXPLORE

- What does hyperconnectivity look like for your brand and how does energy flow across the networks?
- What brands are part of your brand's ecosystem and what core idea defines that ecosystem?
- Draw a map of your ecosystem members and define the roles they play.
- What ecosystems are adjacent to your brand, and what are their core ideas?
- Is there another ecosystem that you would like your brand to be in and how might you get there?

14

Seven Steps to Bring More Enchantment into Your Life

NURTURING ENCHANTMENT IN YOUR LIFE

ENCHANTMENT IS A LITTLE LIKE LOVE. YOU CAN JUST FALL into it and be enthralled. But unlike love, which involves a magical chemistry with another, you can experience enchantment on your own in everyday life. You just have to channel into it. Since many of us have been living unenchanted lives, we likely have hidden barriers that numb receptivity to enchantment. There are simple ways to remove or at least reduce those barriers. So, this chapter is for you.

To access greater enchantment in our own life, you can take some simple steps that I developed which help me navigate several transformative life events, I developed these "seven steps to a more enchanting life" because I needed to "do" things that would work. I share them with you as they will make your journey to creating an Enchanted Brand, culture and company easier, more enjoyable, and also contribute to your own growth.

THE SEVEN STEPS TO AN ENCHANTED LIFE

1. ***Daily Joyful Movement:*** The body may be your snail shell, but it affects you. You need to exert the body physically to keep it alive and heighten the sensitivity of your physical existence. If you haven't moved in years, start slowly and do something that you will enjoy. This not about exercise. It is about joyful movement. Walk and then walk more. Your fitness level actually builds as you move. Step up your game as you move forward. I discovered that cardio dancing was my on ramp. With bad rhythm and no dance ability or experience, I jumped in and found I loved it. Since then, I've added other things, from yoga to weightlifting, that I also enjoy. I always mix it up. Just keep moving. If there is only one thing on this list you do, this is it. Movement is not optional, it is foundational. Try and break a sweat every day. Do joyful movement and you will be hooked for life—little effort or self-discipline needed.

2. ***Embrace Music:*** Music will save your soul. Spotify playlists are awesome. Music helps you surrender and takes your emotions on a ride. It heals in ways we cannot understand. Music can pump you up, assuage a broken heart, reduce loneliness, relax you, let you fly, and even inspire courage. So, be sure to indulge in music frequently and explore a wide variety. Don't just rely on the classics; instead, dare to discover.

3. ***Laugh Once a Day:*** Easier said than done for a serious soul like me, so I really appreciate this one. Some people laugh frequently every day. Not me. This is a skill I had to learn and at which I am getting better. Laughter heals, opens the heart, and pumps magic into our whole life system. Laughter connects us to others and truth. So, try to laugh once a day. A giggle counts. Figure out a "go-to" laugh trigger. I watch a funny YouTube video or *I Love Lucy* episode. It makes an immediate

difference. If I'm lucky, I can focus on thinking about a funny person or event and laugh, but usually I need a real trigger. See if you can work your way to a belly laugh.

4. *Write Your Life:* Take a moment and write your story. Yep. Not a book, just write down your story in words that make sense to you. Past, present, future—one or all. This is why journaling is so powerful and I highly recommend the website Penzu.[125] Just don't live your life, write about it as you live it. This helps you to reflect, understand and tap into instinct and intuition. In writing your story, you will get to know yourself and your circumstances, and gain greater control over both. Ideas, insights, and things you never thought of before, will come to you. This will help you to shape your own life narrative. No one will know you are doing it. Write anything. No rules here. The process will take you in and guide you. Just show up and write.

5. *Awe:* Every day, experience one moment of natural awe. I look up at the night sky before heading to bed. It's that simple. I step outside and look up. When I look up, I am filled with awe at the vastness of the stars and infinite universe. It reminds me of how little I know and how connected I am to things beyond my understanding. When a distant star some trillion miles away gives me a thrill with its bright light, I think, "Wow, that thing a gazillion miles away is shining its light all the way to me and making an impression on me. We are actually in communication." You may find awe in the smile of a baby, a ladybug, waves on an ocean, or the smell of cut grass. Find and embrace it.

6. *Breathe Deep:* Breathing really matters. I wish someone had told me this long ago. Your breath is like water to a drying plant. Be sure to breathe deeply every day. We all live breathing shallow breaths. When you breathe deep, you hydrate yourself. Take it in, hold it, let it out. Do this whenever you can, over and over. When you breathe, it nourishes your existence. Ahhhhhhhhh.

7. *Give:* That one word says it all. Several times a week, authentically give someone something that matters. A hug, your place in line, a loving remark, appreciation—something that is truthful and positive and meets the need of another person. It can be very simple, such as offering directions to someone who is lost instead of passing them by or letting a car go in front of you. Give an extra tip to a great waiter. Tell your friend you love her. Give it and feel the giving. This is not about the response, but about experiencing the giving.

This seven-step process helps get rid of heavy baggage, weeds, clouds, negative self-talk, and other invisible forces standing in the way of more enchantment. If you put your heart into practicing these steps, you will rediscover enchantment within yourself, know what you truly like and don't like and have the strength to make changes and embark on the adventure of your own life. It will help you to live into the future and start again every day fresh as a daisy.

For those seeking an advanced immersion:

Opera: It may feel inaccessible, but you just need to give it a try and dive in. Try *Carmen, Rigoletto.*

Art: Visit a museum. Get to understand art. You can go classic or modern. First just expose yourself and take it one step at a time. Maybe choose one artist and get to understand them. If you can open this world, it is a treasure trove of enchantment.

Poetry: Similar to art and opera, but a very different feeling. Same process.

Play an Instrument: Yes, take the time and learn how to play an instrument. Maybe become a campfire ukelele player like me.

Draw or Paint: Take the time to learn how to draw or paint just for the experience.

15

Building a Better World with Enchanted Brands

ENCHANTED BRANDS ARE PART OF THE BLUEPRINT FOR A better world where brands and brand experiences strengthen humanity and enable us to grow and evolve during metamorphosis. We are in a unique moment in our evolution, when change has accelerated almost beyond comprehension, and global interconnectivity has supported constant disruption. With the new essentialism, we have a new global consciousness on which to shift focus from problem to possibility. We must ride the possibilities of the new world and not cling to the comforts of the current one which is falling away underneath us. Enchanted Brands help us to grow and not shrink during this daunting time. They stimulate our imaginations to fuel greater human energy in the world, help us to be more human, and deepen our experience of life. They leverage the world of business and commerce as a delivery system to shape culture and integrate businesses into our lives as meaningful players in our struggle to evolve. Enchanted Brands bring us all together and align us with the new essentialism. They are a link to grow the corporate and human heart and inspire business and personal minds to see new possibilities and adapt. Ultimately, they help people to enjoy more of what it is to be human in our brave new world and businesses to better grow from helping humanity thrive during a time of epochal change.

We all recognize that we are in a unique moment in our evolution, when change has accelerated almost beyond comprehension, and global connectivity has gone broad and deep, creating both challenges and opportunities that are complex and emergent. If we want to have agency—creating new things and shaping change—in complex, radically contingent contexts, we need to think in terms of how to be human and grow within complex systems. If we start building Enchanted Brands that liberate the imagination, humanity will be stronger, live more deeply, have greater resilience, and may very well evolve into a higher level of experience.

In building an Enchanted Brand, we must listen deeply with our hearts to hear the background sounds, and we must look intensely to see underlying dynamics. We can use stillness to amplify listening and to mobilize the imagination. We can create quiet spaces that become spaces of permission: permission to listen and assimilate context; permission to imagine without repercussions; permission to play with possibilities in order to test them, test boundaries and constraints; permission not to know what we are doing all the time; permission to start anew.

While being responsible to real-world constraints, we can hold real-world constraints at bay in order to see things differently, understand more deeply, and trick the too-often elusive imagination into service. Ideally, Enchanted Brands allow us to shift focus from problem to possibility, often rendering certain immovable objects irrelevant.

With the new essentialism, we have a new global consciousness on which to build.

The occurrence of unexpected events and the dynamic interaction of ecologies in complex contexts, all affirm that direct causality is, at best, only an approximation of a way to understand reality. We need to shape, not control, and influence rather than determine.

Change is going to spring from the heart and the imagination, and Enchanted Brands not only awaken both, they constantly reinforce and nurture the ability to dream and think anew. As a result, they stabilize, and give people comfort that they can deal with the new and not have to be disrupted every time an unthinkable event happens. They have to work *with* constant change and find joy in it. To do this we need to build new human capabilities.

With the new essentialism, humanity is evolving. Greater thought, care and deliberation are embedded into life, and there is a commitment to growth and renewal. This new consciousness will embrace Enchanted Brands, because both feed off of creating new possibilities. Sometimes fixing the old happens when you simply create the new.

As leaders, let us not waste the opportunity to better serve the human side of business and embrace our company's role in the system of life. All we have to do is care and commit. Give people greater agency in the world and be part of that agency. Create brands that partner rather than sell. Recognize the singularity of our hyperconnected society—especially commerce and communications. Know there is an awakening underway in which you can use an Enchanted Brand to produce greater economic, social, and personal value.

CHARACTERISTICS OF THE NEW WORLD

In our new world, people are increasingly marginalized by revolutionizing technologies that dehumanize and distort reality. From constant algorithmic communications to digital tracking and privacy invasions to using our profiles to echo our own ideas (creating the illusion and delusion that the whole world shares our ideas) to automatically making decisions for us and telling us what they think we want to hear (yes, Alexa, that's you), we are being subjugated, manipulated, and played. In addition, pandemic communications, social distancing, and remote working have made physical proximity a fatal risk, further separating us. What happens when we live without hugs, kisses, high fives, fist bumps, and handshakes?

Our complex society that is too hard to understand is endlessly surprising us. History is continuously being rewritten, revealing new truths. It's hard to know what's real and what's not. Who are we? Where do we come from? Where are we going? What matters? Personal, familial, community, national, and global identity matter, and metamorphosis puts those identities into motion.

Over the next decade, we will experience massive social and cultural change, which will result in a complete overhaul of how we do business. When combining the dynamics of people and the internet, ubiquitous connected devices and systems, the dark web, alternate currencies, artificial intelligence (AI) with big data, global interconnectedness, ubiquitous computing, the digitization of matter, new modes of manufacturing (e.g., three-dimensional printing), and the sharing economy (with the barter and gifting economy), it's easy to see how different the world is becoming. There will be persistent disruptions causing disequilibrium, increasing divergence and diffusion, shifts in power and ownership, virtual and augmented living, a significant automated workforce, and time compression.

The fundamental change in the human experience of time is the most startling. Although much of what will happen is unknowable, this scenario demands a new way of thinking about business, society, and culture. Business leaders are learning that much of their success depends on sensing and addressing the rapidly shifting values, expectation and demands of their many stakeholders—the human side of business.

With metamorphosis, the world is shifting in all social, material and mental domains:

- New technologies increasing amount and complexity of challenges and opportunities.

- Exponential rate of change making it critical to adapt with agility.
- Non-linear cause and effects: causes and effects are not sequentially bound together.

New rules govern this new world. Instant change can come from many surprising places. What really matters is often hidden where usual experts don't or can't easily look. The speed of networks outstrips the velocity of decisions. Tiny forces can have immense impacts. Perhaps most importantly, objects are changed by connection. In this new world, the power of the imagination, play, speculative and experimental thinking, non-linear reasoning, instincts, insights, and intuition are more helpful than the historical model of analytical, empirical reasoning. This is why Enchanted Brands, which are fueled by the imagination, will have greater traction than traditional brands.

ENCHANTED BRANDS BRING
THE POWER OF ART

"Imagination is not an embellishment or adjacency to real work in the world, but the keystone capacity upon which all other work depends because it supports sense making, and advances empathy, as much as it drives novelty.[126]

The more extreme the novelty, the more the imagination must work in the process of reasoning.[127]
— Ann M. Pendleton-Jullian and John Seely Brown, Design Unbound

THE ENCHANTED BRAND

"Imagination is more important than knowledge. Knowledge is limited. Imagination encircles the world."
— **Albert Einstein, 1929**[130]

When it comes to feeling our humanity and understanding human truths, art has always captured it. Since the beginning of civilization—music, painting, sculpture, dance, stories, and so on—have told the human story in ways that are meaningful and endure. It is through art that we can rebuild our society amidst the angst and risks of metamorphosis so that humanity is not lost or diminished, but rather is deepened and grows through the process.

Brands are a form of public art. Given the almost trillion dollars spent on them annually on a global basis, they speak loudly and touch many. They contribute to culture and social knowledge, although have not been held accountable for that role. Companies have been allowed to ignore the social and cultural consequences of their branding and have focused solely on the business return-on-investment of the brand. Many brands have polluted and shamelessly exploited with no regard for damage (think of beauty brands setting unrealistic beauty standards or household product brands defining the characters of a "good" home or parent). I believe these companies need to accept that their brands play an important role in the social and cultural fabric, and therefore can make a profound positive difference during this turbulent time. The clarion call for Enchanted Brands is to embrace this responsibility and deliberately to create brands that act as positive social agents helping humanity to cope, thrive, grow, and evolve in our new world.

In this regard, Enchanted Brands represent a pivot from traditional brands. While brands have always been public art, they have been created and leveraged largely to exploit society rather than contribute to it. The more than $240 billion spent each year globally has consequences that are not measured, and no one has accountability. Enchanted Brands aim to end this brand pollution, and to create brands that serve rather than sell, and for brands to be an extension of a company's responsibility to act with mindfulness for the greater good. This aligns with the new essentialism and enables companies to manage the volatile human side of business.

Most of us know the feeling of being moved by a work of art, whether it is a song, a play, a poem, a novel, or a painting. When we are touched, we are moved; we are transported to a new place that is, nevertheless, strongly rooted in a physical experience, in our bodies. We become aware of a feeling that may not be unfamiliar to us but which we did not actively focus on before. This transformative experience is what art is constantly seeking, and it is also what Enchanted Brands aim to achieve.

I believe that one of the major responsibilities of brands is to help people not only get to know and understand something with their minds but also to feel it emotionally and physically. By doing this, brands can mitigate the numbing effect created by the glut of information we are faced with today, and motivate people to think, feel, and create.

Like arts and culture, brands represent one of the few areas in our society where people can come together to share an experience even if they see the world in radically different ways. The important thing is not that we agree about the brand we share, but that we consider it worthwhile to share an experience at all. Brands can be a form of cultural expression where disagreement is accepted and embraced as an essential ingredient. In this sense, the community created by brands is potentially a great source of inspiration for those who want to transcend the polarizing populism and stigmatization of other people, positions, and worldviews that is sadly so endemic in public discourse today.

Like art, brands can also encourage us to cherish intuition, uncertainty, and creativity and to search constantly for new ideas. Artists aim to break rules and find unorthodox ways of approaching contemporary issues. For example, Ai Weiwei, the great Chinese artist, is currently making a temporary studio on the island of Lesbos to draw attention to the plight of the millions of migrants trying to enter Europe right now and also to create a point of contact that takes us beyond an us-and-them mentality to a broader idea of what constitutes "we." This is one way that art can engage with the world to change the world. Enchanted Brands can act in similar ways to make the world a better place.

AN ENCHANTED BRAND TO INSPIRE

A good example of an Enchanted Brand is Little Sun, a solar energy project and social business established in 2012. On a practical level, the company promotes solar energy for all by producing and distributing affordable solar-powered lamps and mobile chargers, focusing especially on reaching regions of the world that do not have consistent access to an electrical grid. At the same time, the Little Sun brand is also about making people feel connected to the lives of others in places that are far away geographically. For those who pick up a Little Sun solar lamp, hold it in their hands, and use it to light their evening, the lamp communicates a feeling of having resources and of being powerful. With Little Sun, a person taps into the energy of the sun to power up with solar energy. It takes something that belongs to all of us—the sun—and makes it available to each of us. This feeling of having personal power is something we can all identify with, and it gives us a feeling of agency in the world. Little Sun creates a community based around this feeling that spans the globe.

Enchanted Brands can cross borders and barriers to bring us together to share and discuss and help to make us more tolerant of differences. The encounter with the brand—and with others over the brand—can help us identify with one another, expand our notions of "we," and show us that individual engagement in the world has actual consequences. That's why I hope that in the future, Enchanted Brands will take a significant role in discussions of social, political, and ecological issues.

Nike kickstarted the inner athlete in all of us and helped fuel the fitness revolution. Apple unleashed our inner creativity and enabled us to make things we never knew we could. The Marines combines duty, honor and extreme strength to create ultimate warriorship. Chanel challenges us to discover and redefine feminine beauty constantly. All of these brands take us places, engage our imaginations, and enable us to think and feel outside of our usual realm.

As society radically metamorphosizes, Enchanted Brands can play a vital role in preserving and nurturing humanity by acting as a trigger of cultural memory. Cultural memory is the act of transfer whereby individuals and groups constitute their identities by recalling a shared past on the basis of common stories and habits. Although he does not use the term "collective memory," French sociologist David Émile Durkheim noted how societies require continuity and connection with the past in order to preserve social unity and cohesion.[128] In his study on traditional religious rituals, collective memory played the role of social pacifier. For French philosopher and sociologist Maurice Halbwachs, the same memory is mediated and constructed by historical events, dramatic happenings or personal memories that are formed, kept and connected.[129] Because personal memory is inherently contestable, in order to validate it, we put forward a process of knitting our disjointed recollections into narratives, revising personal components to fit the collectively remembered past, and gradually cease to distinguish between them. Therefore, collective memory is always a mediated memory, a product of the interplay of experiences conveyed and manipulated through practices and media that transfer as well as transform memory. Enchanted Brands are vehicles to trigger that memory.

When Enchanted Brands interact with the world's peripheries, often characterized by hyper-diverse settlements intertwined with the local collective memory, they have the opportunity to operate as a platform for sharing and debate, and to act as a catalyst toward the co-creation of a common destiny that includes the voices of the voiceless.

Like art, brands are artifacts of humanity that keep us moored together and feeling our humanity. They are reflections of human needs, wants and dreams. By igniting imagination, Enchanted Brands will help humanity to think the unthinkable, entertain the nonviable, and revel in boundary-pushing, domain-jumping, and disruption.

TAKEAWAYS

- In metamorphosis, society needs rebuilding with human care.
- Humanity is at risk, and actions must be taken to strengthen it, deepen it.
- Art is a uniquely human product that conveys truth in universal, personal, and enduring ways, and is part of how we rebuild society as we want it to be.
- Brands are public and have a responsibility to help humanity during this turbulent time.
- Enchanted Brands are public art, with the aim of connecting, transforming, and elevating people.
- Enchanted Brands serve people rather than sell to them, and in serving create a relevant commitment and connection with them.

QUESTIONS TO EXPLORE

- How has the human experience in your company evolved over time?
- How has your brand contributed to the culture?
- If your brand today is an artifact, what does it say about humanity?

Bibliography

Adler, Margot. "Behind the Ever-Expanding American Dream House." NPR.org, July 4, 2006. https://www.npr.org/templates/story/story.php?storyId=5525283.

Alcorn, Chauncey. "US Billionaires' Fortunes Skyrocketed $845 Billion Since March." CNN, September 17, 2020. https://www.cnn.com/2020/09/17/business/us-billionaire-wealth-increase-pandemic/index.html.

Augustine, Kaitlin. "Americans Aren't Minimalists, But Some Aspire to Be." *CivicScience*, August 27, 2018. https://civicscience.com/americans-arent-minimalists/.

Baer, Drake. "How Only Being Able to Use Logic to Make Decisions Destroyed a Man's Life." *The Cut*, June 14, 2016. https://www.thecut.com/2016/06/how-only-using-logic-destroyed-a-man.html.

Bartik, Alexander W., Zoë Cullen, Edward L. Glaeser, Michael Luca, and Christopher Stanton. "What Jobs Are Being Done at Home During the COVID-19 Crisis? Evidence from Firm-Level Surveys." *Harvard Business School Entrepreneurial Management Working Papers* 20, no. 138 (July 29, 2020): 27.

Baumgartner, Natalie. "Build a Culture That Aligns with People's Values." *Harvard Business Review*, April 8, 2020. https://hbr.org/2020/04/build-a-culture-that-aligns-with-peoples-values.

Beck, Ulrich. *The Metamorphosis of the World: How Climate Change Is Transforming Our Concept of the World*. Cambridge, UK: Polity Press, 2016.

Becker, Joshua. "Why We Buy More Than We Need." Forbes, November 27, 2018. https://www.forbes.com/sites/joshua-becker/2018/11/27/why-we-buy-more-than-we-need/.

Bhattarai, Abha. "Now Hiring, for a One-Day Job: The Gig Economy Hits Retail." *Washington Post*, May 4, 2018, sec. Business. https://www.washingtonpost.com/business/economy/now-hiring-for-a-one-day-job-the-gig-economy-hits-retail/2018/05/04/2bebdd3c-4257-11e8-ad8f-27a8c409298b_story.html.

"Bruno Bettelheim: American Psychologist." In Encyclopedia Britannica, March 10, 2021. https://www.britannica.com/biography/Bruno-Bettelheim.

Cameron, Nadia. "How National Geographic Is Innovating Its Brand with Purpose." *CMO Australia*, March 23, 2017. https://www.cmo.com.au/article/616491/how-national-geographic-building-brand-purpose-led-future/.

Carr, Sam. "How Many Ads Do We See a Day?" P*PC Protect*, February 15, 2021. https://ppcprotect.com/how-many-ads-do-we-see-a-day/.

Carroll, Lewis. *Alice's Adventures in Wonderland and Through the Looking Glass*. Reader's Library Classics, 2021.

Casey, Maud. T*he Art of Mystery: The Search for Questions*. Graywolf Press, 2018.

Castells, Manuel. *The Rise of the Network Society*. 2nd ed. Chichester, UK: Wiley-Blackwell, 2010.

Choi, Audrey. "How Younger Investors Could Reshape the World." Morgan Stanley, January 24, 2018. https://www.morganstanley.com/access/why-millennial-investors-are-different.

ClinCalc.com. "Alprazolam: Drug Usage Statistics, United States, 2008 - 2018," January 18, 2021. https://clincalc.com/DrugStats/Drugs/Alprazolam.

Dailymail.com. "Women Spend Eight Years of Their Life Shopping," November 27, 2006. https://www.dailymail.co.uk/fe-mail/article-419077/Women-spend-years-life-shopping.html.

Damasio, Antonio R. Descartes' Error: *Emotion, Reason, and the Human Brain*. New York: Penguin, 1994.

Davidson, Lauren. "British Workers Are Skipping Lunch and That's Hurting Productivity." *The Telegraph*, January 6, 2015. https://www.telegraph.co.uk/finance/jobs/11326076/British-workers-are-skipping-lunch-and-thats-hurting-productivity.html.

Debt.org. "The U.S. Consumer Debt Crisis," January 28, 2021. https://www.debt.org/faqs/americans-in-debt/.

Deloitte. "Culture of Purpose." Accessed March 23, 2021. https://www2.deloitte.com/us/en/pages/about-deloitte/articles/culture-of-purpose.html.

Denizet-Lewis, Benoit. "Why Are More American Teenagers Than Ever Suffering From Severe Anxiety?" *The New York Times*, October 11, 2017, sec. Magazine. https://www.nytimes.com/2017/10/11/magazine/why-are-more-american-teenagers-than-ever-suffering-from-severe-anxiety.html.

Dewar, Carolyn, Martin Hirt, and Scott Keller. "The Mindsets and Practices of Excellent CEOs." MicKinsey & Company, October 25, 2019. http://ceros.mckinsey.com/the-next-normal-callout.

Duffin, Erin. "Total Number of Patents Issued in the U.S. FY 2000-FY 2020." *Statista*, November 19, 2020. https://www.statista.com/statistics/256571/number-of-patent-grants-in-the-us/.

Durkheim, Émile. *The Elementary Forms of Religious Life*. Translated by Carol Cosman. Oxford: Oxford University Press, 2008.

Dwoskin, Elizabeth. "Americans Might Never Go Back to the Office, and Twitter Is Leading the Charge." *The Washington Post*, October 1, 2020, sec. Technology. https://www.washingtonpost.com/technology/2020/10/01/twitter-work-from-home/.

Faith Popcorn's BrainReserve. "TrendBank." Accessed March 23, 2021. https://faithpopcorn.com/trendbank/.

Fitzgerald, Maggie. "U.S. Savings Rate Hits Record 33% as Coronavirus Causes Americans to Stockpile Cash, Curb Spending." CNBC, May 29, 2020. https://www.cnbc.com/2020/05/29/us-savings-rate-hits-record-33percent-as-coronavirus-causes-americans-to-stockpile-cash-curb-spending.html.

Friedman, Thomas L. *Thank You for Being Late: An Optimist's Guide to Thriving in the Age of Accelerations.* 2nd ed. New York: Picador, 2017.

Frisch, Benjamin, and Willa Paskin. "Decoder Ring: The Incunabula Papers: What Lies at the Heart of Ong's Hat?" *Slate*, October 29, 2018. https://slate.com/culture/2018/10/decoder-ring-explores-the-interdimensional-conspiracy-theory-known-as-ongs-hat-the-man-who-created-it-and-the-new-form-of-art-it-birthed.html.

Fuller, Jack, Michael G. Jacobides, and Martin Reeves. "The Myths and Realities of Business Ecosystems." *MIT Sloan Management Review*, February 25, 2019. https://sloanreview.mit.edu/article/the-myths-and-realities-of-business-ecosystems/.

Gaiman, Neil. *The Books of Magic.* 30th Anniversary Edition. Burbank, CA: DC Comics, 2019.

Ganti, Akhilesh. "Economic Moat." Investopedia, March 21, 2020. https://www.investopedia.com/terms/e/economicmoat.asp.

Gardner, Colton. "Self Storage Industry Statistics (2020)." *Neighbor Blog* (blog), December 18, 2019. https://www.neighbor.com/storage-blog/self-storage-industry-statistics/.

Ghaffary, Shirin. "Facebook Is the Latest Major Tech Company to Let People Work from Home Forever." *Vox*, May 21, 2020. https://www.vox.com/recode/2020/5/21/21266570/facebook-remote-work-from-home-mark-zuckerberg-twitter-covid-19-coronavirus.

Gilchrist, Karen. "These Millennials Are Reinventing the Multi-billion-Dollar Education Industry during Coronavirus." CNBC, June 8, 2020. https://www.cnbc.com/2020/06/08/edtech-how-schools-education-industry-is-changing-under-coronavirus.html.

Gillis, Andrew S. "What Is the Gig Economy?" WhatIs.com. Accessed March 24, 2021. https://whatis.techtarget.com/definition/gig-economy.

Gioia, Dana. "Gioia to Graduates: 'Trade Easy Pleasures for More Complex and Challenging Ones.'" Stanford Report, June 17, 2007. http://news.stanford.edu/news/2007/june20/gradtrans-062007.html.

GradSchools.com. "How Many Ads Do You See Each Day?" September 12, 2018. https://www.gradschools.com/degree-guide/how-many-ads-do-you-see-each-day.

Graham, John R., Campbell R. Harvey, Jillian Popadak, and Shivaram Rajgopal. "Corporate Culture: Evidence from the Field." National Bureau of Economic Research, March 20, 2017. https://www.nber.org/papers/w23255.

Halbwachs, Maurice. *On Collective Memory.* Translated by Lewis A. Coser. Chicago: University of Chicago Press, 1992.

Heartney, Eleanor. "Spirituality Has Long Been Erased From Art History. Here's Why It's Having a Resurgence Today." *Artnet News*, January 6, 2020. https://news.artnet.com/art-world/spirituality-and-art-resurgence-1737117.

Holman, Peggy. *Engaging Emergence: Turning Upheaval into Opportunity.* San Francisco, CA: Berrett-Koehler Publishers, 2010.

Holtz-Eakin, Douglas, Ben Gitis, and Will Rinehart. "The Gig Economy: Research and Policy Implications of Regional, Economic, and Demographic Trends." Future of Work Initiative & American Action Forum. The Aspen Institute, January 2017. https://www.aspeninstitute.org/wp-content/uploads/2017/02/Regional-and-Industry-Gig-Trends-2017.pdf.

Inc.com. "Brands and Brand Names," May 1, 2021. https://www.inc. com/encyclopedia/brands-and-brand-names.html.

Insurance Journal. "GEICO's Advertising Spending Slows but Still Tops $1 Billion: SNL," March 20, 2014. https://www.insurance-journal.com/news/national/2014/03/20/323788.htm.

Intercollegiate Studies Institute ISI Archive. "Why Myth Matters," April 21, 2014. https://isi.org/intercollegiate-review/why-myth-matters/.

James, William. *The Varieties of Religious Experience: A Study in Human Nature*. Centenary Edition. London; New York: Routledge, 2002.

Jameson, Fredric. *The Geopolitical Aesthetic: Cinema and Space in the World System*. Bloomington: Indiana University Press, 1992.

Johnson, Emma. "The Real Cost of Your Shopping Habits." *Forbes*, January 15, 2015. https://www.forbes.com/sites/emmajohnson/2015/01/15/the-real-cost-of-your-shopping-habits/.

Jung, C. G. *Collected Works of C. G. Jung*. Edited by Gerhard Adler and R. F. C. Hull. 2nd ed. Vol. 9 (Part 1): "Archetypes and the Collective Unconscious". Princeton: Princeton University Press, 2014.

Kavanagh, Jennifer, and Michael D. Rich. Truth Decay: An Initial Exploration of the Diminishing Role of Facts and Analysis in American Public Life. Rand Corporation, 2018.

Kawasaki, Guy. "Are You a CEO...'Chief Enchantment Officer'??" Vistage Research Center, January 26, 2012. https://www.vistage.com/research-center/personal-development/leadership-competencies/are-you-a-ceo-chief-enchantment-officer/.

Kawasaki, Guy. *Enchantment: The Art of Changing Hearts, Minds, and Actions*. New York: Penguin, 2011.

Kinder, Marsha. *Playing With Power in Movies, Television, and Video Games: From Muppet Babies to Teenage Mutant Ninja Turtles*. University of California Press, 1991.

Kraaijenbrink, Jeroen. "What Does VUCA Really Mean?" *Forbes,* December 19, 2018. https://www.forbes.com/sites/jeroenkraaijenbrink/2018/12/19/what-does-vuca-really-mean/.

LaFrance, Adrienne. "The Prophecies of Q." *The Atlantic,* June 2020. https://www.theatlantic.com/magazine/archive/2020/06/qanon-nothing-can-stop-what-is-coming/610567/.

Lee, Kyu. "Finland Again Is the Happiest Country in the World," March 20, 2019. https://worldhappiness.report/blog/finland-again-is-the-happiest-country-in-the-world/.

Leonhardt, David, and Stuart A. Thompson. "How Working-Class Life Is Killing Americans, in Charts." *The New York Times,* March 6, 2020, sec. Opinion. https://www.nytimes.com/interactive/2020/03/06/opinion/working-class-death-rate.html.

Leonhardt, Megan. "55% of Americans with Credit Cards Have Debt—Here's How Much It Could Cost You." CNBC, May 20, 2019. https://www.cnbc.com/2019/05/17/55-percent-of-americans-have-credit-card-debt.html.

Levine, David. "Are Some Age Groups More Prone to Depression Than Others?" *US News & World Report,* May 2, 2017. https://health.usnews.com/health-care/patient-advice/articles/2017-05-02/are-some-age-groups-more-prone-to-depression-than-others.

Masters, Lt. J. G. Doug. "Night Carrier Qualifications." *Flying,* July 12, 2007. http://www.flyingmag.com/pilot-reports/jets/night-carrier-qualifications/.

McCue, T. J. "57 Million U.S. Workers Are Part Of The Gig Economy." *Forbes,* August 31, 2018. https://www.forbes.com/sites/tjmccue/2018/08/31/57-million-u-s-workers-are-part-of-the-gig-economy/.

McDowell, Alex. "About." USC School of Cinematic Arts | World Building Media Lab. Accessed March 23, 2021. https://worldbuilding.institute/about.

McDowell, Alex. "Alex McDowell, R.D.I." USC School of Cinematic Arts | World Building Media Lab. Accessed March 23, 2021. https://worldbuilding.usc.edu/people/bio/alex-mcdowell/.

Meero. "11 Dos & Donts for Your LinkedIn Profile Picture in 2020." July 16, 2020. https://www.meero.com/en/news/corporate/411/11-Tips-To-Follow-For-The-Perfect-Linkedin-Profile-Picture-In-2019.

Mejia, Zameena. "Harvard's Longest Study of Adult Life Reveals How You Can Be Happier and More Successful." CNBC, March 20, 2018. https://www.cnbc.com/2018/03/20/this-harvard-study-reveals-how-you-can-be-happier-and-more-successful.html.

Mooallem, Jon. "The Self-Storage Self." *The New York Times*, September 2, 2009, sec. Magazine. https://www.nytimes.com/2009/09/06/magazine/06self-storage-t.html.

Moore, James F. "Predators and Prey: A New Ecology of Competition." *Harvard Business Review,* June 1993. https://hbr.org/1993/05/predators-and-prey-a-new-ecology-of-competition.

Moore, James F. *The Death of Competition: Leadership and Strategy in the Age of Business Ecosystems.* New York: HarperBusiness, 1996.

Mulcahy, Diane. "Who Wins in the Gig Economy, and Who Loses." *Harvard Business Review*, October 27, 2016. https://hbr.org/2016/10/who-wins-in-the-gig-economy-and-who-loses.

Myers, N. "Consumption in Relation to Population, Environment and Development." *The Environmentalist* 17, no. 1 (1997): 33–44.

Northeastern University Graduate Programs. "Tips for Building Your Personal brand," January 14, 2019. https://www.northeastern.edu/graduate/blog/tips-for-building-your-personal-brand/.

Nowak, Martin A. "Five Rules for the Evolution of Cooperation." *Science* 314, no. 5805 (December 8, 2006): 1560–63.

Nye, Joseph S., Jr. *Soft Power: The Means to Success in World Politics.* New York: PublicAffairs, 2005.

Orwall, Bruce, Brian Steinberg, and Joann S. Lublin. "Eisner Steps Down as Disney Chairman." *The Wall Street Journal,* March 4, 2004, sec. News. https://www.wsj.com/articles/SB107832734296045356.

Otto, Rudolf. Autobiographical and Social Essays. Edited by Gregory D. Alles. Berlin: Walter de Gruyter, 1996.

Paz, Octavio. *The Siren and the Seashell: And Other Essays on Poets and Poetry.* Translated by Lysander Kemp and Margaret Sayers Peden. Austin: University of Texas Press, 2013.

Pendleton-Jullian, Ann M. Design Education and Innovation Ecotones, 2009. https://vdocuments.mx/design-education-and-innovation-ecotones-in-the-sciences-technology-and-culture.html.

Pendleton-Julian, Ann M. "Mapping the Pragmatic Imagination: An Interview with Ann M. Pendleton-Jullian (Part Two)". Interview by Henry Jenkins, November 21, 2016. http://henryjenkins.org/blog/2016/11/mapping-the-pragmatic-imagination-an-interview-with-ann-m-pendleton-jullian-part-two.html.

Pendleton-Jullian, Ann M., and John Seely Brown. *Design Unbound: Designing for Emergence in a White Water World.* 2 vols. Cambridge, MA: MIT Press, 2018.

Psychology Today. "Spirituality." Accessed March 22, 2021. https://www.psychologytoday.com/us/basics/spirituality.

Ramo, Joshua Cooper. *The Age of the Unthinkable: Why the New World Disorder Constantly Surprises Us and What We Can Do about It.* New York; Boston; London: Little, Brown and Company, 2009.

Ramo, Joshua Cooper. *The Seventh Sense: Power, Fortune, and Survival in the Age of Networks.* New York; Boston; London: Little, Brown and Company, 2016.

Rehak, Judith. "Tylenol Made a Hero of Johnson & Johnson: The Recall That Started Them All." *The New York Times*, March 23, 2002, sec. Your Money. https://www.nytimes.com/2002/03/23/your-money/IHT-tylenol-made-a-hero-of-johnson-johnson-the-recall-that-started.html.

Renjen, Punit. "What Really Drives Employee Engagement?" ChiefExecutive.net, January 24, 2013. https://chiefexecutive.net/what-really-drives-employee-engagement/.

Retail Dive. "The Running List of 2020 Retail Bankruptcies," February 5, 2021. https://www.retaildive.com/news/the-running-list-of-2020-retail-bankruptcies/571159/.

Rogers, Edward S. "Some Historical Matter Concerning Trade-Marks." *Michigan Law Review* 9, no. 1 (1910): 29–43. https://doi.org/10.2307/1276308.

Samsung. "Samsung Electronics Becomes Top Five in Interbrand's Best Global Brands 2020," October 20, 2020. https://news.samsung.com/global/samsung-electronics-becomes-top-five-in-interbrands-best-global-brands-2020.

Scheer, Roddy, and Doug Moss. "Use It and Lose It: The Outsize Effect of U.S. Consumption on the Environment." *Scientific American*, September 14, 2012. https://www.scientificamerican.com/article/american-consumption-habits/.

Schultz, Howard. *Pour Your Heart into It: How Starbucks Built a Company One Cup at a Time.* New York: Hachette Books, 2012.

Simon & Garfunkel. Bridge Over Troubled Water. New York: Columbia Records, 1970.

Sims, Maja Pawinska. "CEOs Play a Crucial Role in Enhancing & Maintaining Brand Value, Global Study Finds." *PRovoke*, January 24, 2019. https://www.provokemedia.com/latest/article/ceos-play-a-crucial-role-in-enhancing-maintaining-brand-value-global-study-finds.

Singer, Matt. "Welcome to the 2015 Recruiter Nation, Formerly Known as the Social Recruiting Survey." *Jobvite,* September 22, 2015. https://www.jobvite.com/blog/ jobvite-news-and-reports/welcome-to-the-2015-recruiter-nation-formerly-known-as-the-social-recruiting-survey/.

Smith, Aaron. "Gig Work, Online Selling and Home Sharing." Pew Research Center: Internet & Technology, November 17, 2016. https://www.pewresearch.org/internet/2016/11/17/gig-work-online-selling-and-home-sharing/.

Sorenson, Susan, and Keri Garman. "How to Tackle U.S. Employees' Stagnating Engagement." Gallup.com, June 11, 2013. https:// news.gallup.com/businessjournal/162953/tackle-employ-ees-stagnating-engagement.aspx.

Staffing Industry Analysts. "Total Spending on US Gig Work Close to $800 Billion." *PR Newswire,* September 21, 2016. https://www. prnewswire.com/news-releases/total-spending-on-us-gig-work-close-to-800-billion-300331650.html.

Statista. "Global Advertising Spending 2019," March 1, 2021. https://www.statista.com/statistics/236943/global-advertis-ing-spending/.

Stevanovic, Ivan. "How Many ECommerce Sites Are There in 2020?" *KommandoTech* (blog), February 13, 2020. https://kommando-tech.com/statistics/how-many-ecommerce-sites-are-there/.

Strum, Jonathan. "The Big Benzo: Unpacking Xanax Use in Amer-ica." The Recovery Village Drug and Alcohol Rehab, October 5, 2020. https://www.therecoveryvillage.com/drug-addiction/ news/use-in-america/.

United States Congress Joint Economic Committee. "Long-Term Trends in Deaths of Despair." Social Capital Project. Wash-ington, D.C., November 5, 2019. https://www.jec.senate.gov/ public/_cache/files/0f2d3dba-9fdc-41e5-9bd1-9c13f4204e35/ jec-report-deaths-of-despair.pdf.

Vault.com. "Johnson & Johnson." Accessed March 23, 2021. https://www.vault.com/company-profiles/personal-care/johnson-johnson.

Viereck, George Sylvester. "What Life Means to Einstein." *The Saturday Evening Post*. October 26, 1929. http://www.saturdayeveningpost.com/wp-content/uploads/satevepost/what_life_means_to_einstein.pdf.

Vogler, Christopher. *The Writer's Journey: Mythic Structure for Writers*. 3rd ed. Studio City, CA: Michael Wiese Productions, 2007.

Wallander, Mattias. "Closet Cast-Offs Clogging Landfills." *The Huffington Post*, May 25, 2011. https://www.huffpost.com/entry/closet-cast-offs-clogging_b_554400.

Weber, Max. *The Rational and Social Foundations of Music*. Translated by Don Martindale, Johannes Riedel, and Gertrude Neuwirth. Carbondale: Southern Illinois University Press, 1958.

Weir, Peter. Dead Poets Society. Buena Vista Pictures Distribution, 1989.

Whitehouse, Mark. "Number of the Week: Americans Buy More Stuff They Don't Need." *Wall Street Journal*, April 23, 2011, sec. Real Time Economics. https://www.wsj.com/articles/BL-REB-13793.

Wigmore, Ivy. "What Is Flexible Workforce?" WhatIs.com, September 1, 2016. https://whatis.techtarget.com/definition/flexible-workforce.

Wikipedia. "Volatility, Uncertainty, Complexity and Ambiguity." February 14, 2021. https://en.wikipedia.org/wiki/Volatility,_uncertainty,_complexity_and_ambiguity.

Willis, A. J. "The Ecosystem: An Evolving Concept Viewed Historically." *Functional Ecology* 11, no. 2 (1997): 268–71.

Zmirak, John. "The Generosity of Tolkien." Crisis Magazine, January 27, 2010. http://www.crisismagazine.com/2010/the-generosity-of-tolkien.

Acknowledgments

TO THE YOUNG WOMAN WHO WORKED HER WAY THROUGH high school and college, thank you for always believing that no matter how hard things got you would always complete the challenge. Your optimism and fearlessness opened adventurous pathways.

To my parents, Ronald Cavalier and Cecelia Mary Mack, thank you for introducing me to enchantment and the power of positive thinking. Anything is possible.

Thank you to my husband Scott Lucas, my high school sweetheart and spouse of thirty-five years. His relentless encouragement (and badgering) drove me to write this book. He still marvels at how much I love branding, listens to all my crazy stories and believes in the power of Enchanted Brands.

I owe a great debt of gratitude to the various business partners I have had over my career who challenged me to grow including Tom DeCerchio, Bryan Buckley, Peter Kim and Michael Bronner, and my early mentor Ella Kelley. To my brand thought partners Larry Volpi and Phil Halyard, thank you for decades of co-creativity in building great brands. Thank you to Joey Cummings for encouraging me to write this book and share my perspective.

Enchanted Brands are only possible when people commit to them. I am grateful to these outstanding leaders who always "got it": Susan Marquis, Sandi Fenwick, Steve Karp, VADM Joseph Dyer, Corinne Basler and Yaron Eitan. Your faith inspired great brands.

Thank you to Justin Lucas, Phoebe Dean Lucas, Halle Lucas, Daniel Lucas and Melanie McMahon Ives whose expertise contributed to the work, and loving support drove me to stay with it. Thank you to Amber Gans Pereira for the amazing cover art and graphics. Enormous gratitude goes to Sarah Dobbs, my right hand at BrightMark since the beginning, whose commitment and loyalty has made it all possible including writing this book. Thank you to Tom Epley who dedicated many painstaking hours to proofing the galley.

To my Beta Xi SDT sisters of Union College, thank you for your pure heart, emotional nakedness and infinite love which always inspires me - Kathy, Nia, Dirtbag, Coops, Dannin, Cod, Ellen, Linda Cavanna, Fy, Barbara D, Janice, D Rose, Kissel and all the other adventurous souls. Immense gratitude to my soul sister Laura Freed Ancona whose unconditional love and faith give me strength, courage and the ability to experience unseen realities.

Finally, thank you to Henry DeVries, Devin DeVries, and the team at Indie Books International for making this dream come true, and for Andrea Chapin for bringing this humble work to the highest level.

Creating brands continues to be my vocation and how I contribute the world. It has been a privilege to have done this work for so long and for so many. I thank all who gave me the opportunity to build brands that make a difference. I believe brands have the power to enrich our lives, open new possibilities and change the world. All we have to do is enchant them.

About The Author

JANE CAVALIER IS A SEASONED BUSINESS LEADER, BRANDER, market strategist, and board member. She has been involved with creating and launching some of the most exciting and prominent brands of our time including Snapple, Qwest, and AT&T Business, and she has rebranded such leading global companies as Exxon/Esso, Motorola, and Samsung. Jane got her start at Doyle Dane Bernbach and went on to build Buckley DeCerchio Cavalier—a creative boutique featured on the cover of the Sunday *New York Times* as one of the top ten most creative ad agencies in America.

As EVP of Strategic Planning at the world's largest advertising agency, McCann Erickson Worldwide, Jane founded The 14th Floor as McCann's entrance into brand consulting and pioneered practices that became industry standards. After a meteoric rise on Madison Avenue and years of pushing the envelope to improve corporate performance within the advertising industry, Jane left to start BrightMark Consulting to more broadly apply branding to build value across global enterprises, private companies, government agencies, nonprofits, and new ventures. BrightMark's clients have included American Express, the U.S. Navy, GE, IBM, Sotheby's, Boston Children's Hospital, CamelBak, US Department of State, Havas Worldwide, and iRobot.

Jane grew up surrounded by art and experienced enchantment in her early life. Her parents were both initially NYC actors. Her father, a lifelong tenor and actor, went on to build a prominent art foundry for bronze castings giving Jane exposure to artists and vision. Driven to make the world a better place and disillusioned by the traditional advertising world, Jane took her bag of branding tricks out of Madison Avenue and boarded BrightMark as a magic carpet to find and help institutions that needed the power of brand to advance their mission.

Jane serves on the boards of the Pardee RAND Graduate School, Nemours Children's Health System, and the American Composers Orchestra. She has taught as an adjunct at the Yale School of Management and NYU's Stern School of Management, and has been a keynote speaker at events and conferences. Along with BrightMark, she publishes a blog with podcasts called *Overhead Space* that reaches over 75,000 leaders and executives each month.

Jane is a deep-thinking strategist, rigorous analyst, and an imaginative, inspired entrepreneur. She married her high school sweetheart and raised three children as a working mom in a small town in Connecticut. When she is not studying the revolutionizing effects of technology on business, people, and society, she explores the night sky with her telescope, raises chickens in her backyard, and loves kayaking, paddle boarding, boating, hiking, scuba diving, and campfires with friends and family.

Now, during a time of momentous cultural changes, spurred in part by the pandemic, global social activism, and climate change, Jane has turned her attention to helping business leaders navigate this new world with her ground-breaking book, *The Enchanted Brand: Strengthening the Human Side of Business.*

TRADEMARKED BRANDS REFERENCED

Accenture® is a registered trademark of Accenture Global Services Limited ACS.

Acura® is a registered trademark of Acura Division of American Honda Motor Company, Inc.

Airbnb® is a registered trademark of Airbnb, Inc.

Alexa® is a registered trademark of Amazon Technologies, Inc.

American Airlines® is a registered trademark of American Airlines, Inc.

American Express® is a registered trademark of American Express Marketing & Development Corporation.

American Idol® is a registered trademark of 19 TV Ltd.

AOL® is a registered trademark of AOL LLC.

Apple® is a registered trademark of Apple Computer, Inc.

AT&T® is a registered trademark of AT&T Corporation.

Avis® is a registered trademark of Avis Budget.

Avon® is a registered trademark of New Avon LLC.

Batman® is a registered trademark of DC Comics.

Bayer® is a registered trademark of Bayer AG.

Behance® is a registered trademark of Adobe Systems Incorporated.

Birds Eye foods® is a registered trademark of Conagra R&F (PF), LLC.

Bitcoin® is a registered trademark of bitFlyer, Inc.

Black Rifle Coffee® is a registered trademark of Black Rifle Coffee Company, LLC.

BMW® is a registered trademark of Bavarian Motor Works AG.

Brooks Brothers® is a registered trademark of Marks & Spencer Services, Inc.

Budweiser® is a registered trademark of Anheuser-Busch.

Burger King® is a registered trademark of The Burger King Corporation.

Campbell's® **Soup** is a registered trademark of CSC Brand LP.

Chanel® is a registered trademark of Chanel.

Club Med® is a registered trademark of Club Mediterranee.

Coca-Cola® is a registered trademark of The Coca-Cola Company.

Corona® is a registered trademark of Grupo Modelo.

Coursera® is a registered trademark of Coursera, Inc.

Culture Vulture® is a registered trademark of Brittany Tilleman.

Dead Poets Society® is a registered trademark of LNJ Ventures LLC.

Dell® is a registered trademark of Dell, Inc.

Deloitte® is a registered trademark of Deloitte Network.

Delta® is a registered trademark of Delta Air Lines, Inc.

Disney® is a registered trademark of Disney Enterprises, Inc..

Dixie Cups® is a registered trademark of GPCP IP Holdings LLC.

DÔEN® is a registered trademark of Communaute LLC.

Dove® is a registered trademark of Mars, Inc.

Dungeons and Dragons® is a registered trademark of Wizards of the Coast LLC.

Dunkin' Donuts® is a registered trademark of DD IP Holder, LLC.

E-ZPass® is a registered trademark of Port Authority of New York and New Jersey.

Equinox® is a registered trademark of Equinox Systems, Inc.

Esso® is a registered trademark of Imperial Oil.

Estée Lauder® is a registered trademark of The Estée Lauder Companies, Inc.

Exxon® is a registered trademark of Exxon Mobil Corporation.

Federal Express® is a registered trademark of Federal Express Corporation.

Fender® is a registered trademark of Fender Musical Instruments Corporation.

Fiji Water® is a registered trademark of Fiji Water Company LLC.

Firestone® is a registered trademark of Bridgestone Brands, LLC.

Four Seasons® is a registered trademark of The Four Seasons Hotel LP.

Frodo Baggins® is a registered trademark of Saul Zaentz Company.

Fujifilm® is a registered trademark of Fujifilm Holdings Corporation.

Gap® is a registered trademark of Gap (Apparel), LLC.

Gatorade® is a registered trademark of Stokely-Van Camp, Inc.

Geico® is a registered trademark of Geico.

Glass® is a registered trademark of Google Inc.

Godfather's Pizza® is a registered trademark of Godfather's Pizza, Inc.

Google® is a registered trademark of Google Inc.

Goop® is a registered trademark of Goop, Inc.

Grey Goose® is a registered trademark of Grey Goose Importing Company.

Hallmark® is a registered trademark of Hallmark Licensing, LLC.

Harley Davidson® is a registered trademark of Harley Davidson Motorcycle Company.

Harry Potter® is a registered trademark of Warner Bros. Entertainment Inc.

Heineken® is a registered trademark of Heineken N.V.

Hertz® is a registered trademark of Hertz System, Inc.

Hewlett-Packard® is a registered trademark of Hewlett-Packard Company.

Honda® is a registered trademark of Honda Motor Corporation.

Huggies® is a registered trademark of Kimberly-Clark.

IBM® is a registered trademark of IBM-Corp.

Igloo® is a registered trademark of Igloo Products Corp.

Instagram® is a registered trademark of Instagram, LLC.

Intel® is a registered trademark of Intel Corporation.

Ivory Soap® is a registered trademark of The Procter & Gamble Company.

J.Crew® is a registered trademark of J. Crew International, Inc.

J.C. Penney® is a registered trademark of Penney IP LLC.

Jeep® is a registered trademark of Chrysler Group LLC.

JetBlue® is a registered trademark of JetBlue Airways Corporation.

John Deere® is a registered trademark of Deere & Company.

Johnson & Johnson® is a registered trademark of Johnson & Johnson, Inc.

Kellogg® is a registered trademark of The Kellogg Company.

Kmart® is a registered trademark of The Kmart Corporation.

Kodak® is a registered trademark of Eastman Kodak Company.

L.S./M.F.T.® is a registered trademark of Reynolds Innovations Inc.

Land Rover® is a registered trademark of Land Rover North America, Inc.

Lego® is a registered trademark of The Lego Group.

LENS® is a registered trademark of Sandia National Labs.

LG® is a registered trademark of LG Electronics, Inc.

LinkedIn® is a registered trademark of LinkedIn Corporation.

LMI® is a registered trademark of Milton Roy, LLC.

Lord & Taylor® is a registered trademark of Lord & Taylor.

Lord of the Rings® is a registered trademark of Saul Zaentz Company.

Lucky Brand® is a registered trademark of Lucky Brand Dungarees, Inc.

Lucky Strike® is a registered trademark of Brown & Williamson Tobacco Corporation.

Luke Skywalker® is a registered trademark of Lucasfilm Entertainment Company LTD.

LuluLemon® is a registered trademark of Lululemon Athletica Canada Inc.

Marlboro® is a registered trademark of Philip Morris USA.

Mastercard® is a registered trademark of MasterCard International.

McDonalds® is a registered trademark of McDonalds Corporation.

MCI® is a registered trademark of MCI Communications Corporation.

McKinsey® is a registered trademark of McKinsey Holdings, Inc.

Mercedes Benz® is a registered trademark of Daimler AG.

Merck® is a registered trademark of Merck & Co., Inc.

Michelin® is a registered trademark of Michelin North America, Inc.

Microsoft® is a registered trademark of Microsoft Corporation.

Miller® is a registered trademark of Miller Brewing Company.

Minority Report® is a registered trademark of Paramount Pictures Corporation.

MTV® is a registered trademark of Viacom International Inc.

Narnia® is a registered trademark of CS Lewis Pte Ltd.

National Geographic® is a registered trademark of National Geographic Society.

NAVAIR® is a registered trademark of The Department of the Navy.

Neiman Marcus® is a registered trademark of NM Nevada Trust.

NetJets® is a registered trademark of NetJets and Berkshire Hathaway.

Newton® is a registered trademark of Apple Computer, Inc.

Nike® is a registered trademark of Nike, Inc.

OpenTable® is a registered trademark of OpenTable LLC.

Oprah® is a registered trademark of Harpo, Inc.

Orvis® is a registered trademark of Orvis, Inc.

Pampers® is a registered trademark of The Procter & Gamble Company.

Pan Am® is a registered trademark of Pan American World Airways, LLC.

Patagonia® is a registered trademark of Patagonia, Inc.

Pella® is a registered trademark of Pella Corporation.

Pepsi® is a registered trademark of PepsiCo, Inc.

Pier 1 Imports® is a registered trademark of Pier 1 Imports Online, Inc.

Play-Doh® is a registered trademark of Hasbro, Inc.

Poland Spring® is a registered trademark of Nestlé Waters North America.

Porsche® is a registered trademark of Porsche AG and Porsche Cars North America.

Prius® is a registered trademark of Toyota Motor Corporation.

Prodigy® is a registered trademark of Prodigy Services Corporation.

Qwest® is a registered trademark of Qwest Communication International Inc.

Ralph Lauren® is a registered trademark of Ralph Lauren Corporation.

RAND® is a registered trademark of RAND Corporation.

RC Cola® is a registered trademark of Royal Crown Cola Company.

REI® is a registered trademark of Recreational Equipment, Inc.

Rocky Mountain Sparkling Water® is a registered trademark of Molson Coors Company.

Samsung® is a registered trademark of Samsung Group.

Satisfries® is a registered trademark of Burger King Corporation.

Shinola® is a registered trademark of Bedrock Brands, LP.

Skillshare® is a registered trademark of Skillshare, Inc.

SmileDirectClub® is a registered trademark of Smile Direct Club, LLC.

Snap, Crackle, Pop® is a registered trademark of The Kellogg Company.

Snickers® is a registered trademark of Mars, Inc.

Sony® is a registered trademark of Sony Corporation.

Southwest Airlines® is a registered trademark of Southwest Airlines, Inc.

Spanx® is a registered trademark of Spanx, Inc.

Sparks & Honey® is a registered trademark of Sparks & Honey LLC.

Spider-Man® is a registered trademark of Marvel Characters, Inc.

Sprint® is a registered trademark of Sprint Corporation.

Star Trek® is a registered trademark of Paramount Pictures.

Star Wars® is a registered trademark of Lucasfilm Entertainment Company LTD.

Starbucks® is a registered trademark of Starbucks Corporation.

Stay Curious® is a registered trademark of John Templeton Foundation.

Sur la Table® is a registered trademark of Sur la Table, Inc.

Surf® is a registered trademark of Unilever, plc.

Suzuki® is a registered trademark of Suzuki Motor Co., Ltd.

Tesla® is a registered trademark of Tesla Motors, Inc.

The Matrix® is a registered trademark of The Wachowskis and Warner Brothers Studios.

The New York Times® is a registered trademark of The New York Times Company.

The Paper Store® is a registered trademark of The Paper Store LLC.

Tide® is a registered trademark of The Procter & Gamble Company.

Tiffany® is a registered trademark of Tiffany & Co.

Toptal® is a registered trademark of Toptal LLC.

Trend Hunter® is a registered trademark of Trend Hunter, Inc.

TripAdvisor® is a registered trademark of TripAdvisor LLC.

True Religion® is a registered trademark of Guru Denim, Inc.

Twitter® is a registered trademark of Twitter, Inc.

Tylenol® is a registered trademark of McNeil Consumer Healthcare.

U.S. Airways® is a registered trademark of American Airlines Group.

Uber® is a registered trademark of Uber Technologies, Inc.

United Airlines® is a registered trademark of United Airlines, Inc.

Venmo® is a registered trademark of PayPal, Inc.

Virgin® is a registered trademark of Virgin Enterprises Limited.

Virgin Air® is a registered trademark of Virgin Enterprises Limited.

Visa® is a registered trademark of Visa International Services Association.

Volvo® is a registered trademark of AB Volvo.

Walmart® is a registered trademark of Wal-Mart Stores, Inc.

Weight Watchers® is a registered trademark of Weight Watchers International.

Whole Foods® is a registered trademark of Amazon Technologies, Inc.

World of Warcraft® is a registered trademark of Blizzard Entertainment, Inc.

WW® is a registered trademark of WW International, Inc.

Xanax® is a registered trademark of Pfizer, Inc.

Yamaha® is a registered trademark of Yamaha Corporation.

Yeti® is a registered trademark of Yeti Coolers, LLC.

Zoom® is a registered trademark of Zoom Video Communications, Inc.

Endnotes

1 For the source of this story involving General Stanley McChrystal, see Ann M. Pendleton-Jullian and John Seely Brown, *Design Unbound: Designing for Emergence in a White Water World* (Cambridge, MA: MIT Press, 2018), 2:290–333.

2 Quoted in Thomas L. Friedman, *Thank You for Being Late: An Optimist's Guide to Thriving in the Age of Accelerations*, 2nd ed. (New York: Picador, 2017), 201.

3 Joshua Cooper Ramo, *The Seventh Sense: Power, Fortune, and Survival in the Age of Networks* (New York; Boston; London: Little, Brown and Company, 2016), Chapter 1, section 2.

4 Ulrich Beck, *The Metamorphosis of the World: How Climate Change Is Transforming Our Concept of the World* (Cambridge, UK: Polity Press, 2016), Chapter 4, section 2, "Metamorphosis."

5 Jeroen Kraaijenbrink, "What Does VUCA Really Mean?," *Forbes*, December 19, 2018, https://www.forbes.com/sites/jeroenkraaijenbrink/2018/12/19/what-does-vuca-really-mean/; "Volatility, Uncertainty, Complexity and Ambiguity," in Wikipedia, February 14, 2021, https://en.wikipedia.org/wiki/Volatility,_uncertainty,_complexity_and_ambiguity.

6 Beck, *The Metamorphosis of the World*, Chapter 1, section 1, "Uniform vs. Diverse Metamorphosis of the World."

7 Beck, Chapter 2, section 4.

8 Beck, Chapter 4, section 2, "Metamorphosis."

9 Beck, Chapter 1, "Note."

10 Quoted in Ann M. Pendleton-Jullian, *Design Education and Innovation Ecotones*, 2009, 56, https://vdocuments.mx/design-education-and-innovation-ecotones-in-the-sciences-technology-and-culture.html.

11 Joshua Cooper Ramo, *The Age of the Unthinkable: Why the New World Disorder Constantly Surprises Us And What We Can Do About It* (New York; Boston; London: Little, Brown and Company, 2009).

[12] Ramo, *The Seventh Sense,* Chapter 2.

[13] Manuel Castells, *The Rise of the Network Society,* 2nd ed. (Chichester, UK: Wiley-Blackwell, 2010), 508; quoted in Ramo, The Seventh Sense, Chapter 4, section 2.

[14] Ramo, *The Seventh Sense,* Chapter 5, section 4, 138.

[15] Peggy Holman, *Engaging Emergence: Turning Upheaval Into Opportunity* (San Francisco, CA: Berrett-Koehler Publishers, 2010), 27.

[16] Ramo, *The Seventh Sense*, Chapter 3, section 2.

[17] Ramo, Chapter 11, section 4.

[18] Sam Carr, "How Many Ads Do We See A Day?," PPC Protect, February 15, 2021, https://ppcprotect.com/how-many-ads-do-we-see-a-day/.

[19] "Global Advertising Spending 2019," *Statista*, March 1, 2021, https://www.statista.com/statistics/236943/global-advertising-spending/.

[20] "The U.S. Consumer Debt Crisis," Debt.org, January 28, 2021, https://www.debt.org/faqs/americans-in-debt/.

[21] Chauncey Alcorn, "US Billionaires' Fortunes Skyrocketed $845 Billion Since March," CNN, September 17, 2020, https://www.cnn.com/2020/09/17/business/us-billionaire-wealth-increase-pandemic/index.html.

[22] Kyu Lee, "Finland Again Is the Happiest Country in the World," March 20, 2019, https://worldhappiness.report/blog/finland-again-is-the-happiest-country-in-the-world/.

[23] Joshua Becker, "Why We Buy More Than We Need," *Forbes*, November 27, 2018, https://www.forbes.com/sites/joshuabecker/2018/11/27/why-we-buy-more-than-we-need/.

[24] Mark Whitehouse, "Number of the Week: Americans Buy More Stuff They Don't Need," *Wall Street Journal*, April 23, 2011, sec. Real Time Economics, https://www.wsj.com/articles/BL-REB-13793.

[25] N. Myers, "Consumption in Relation to Population, Environment and Development," *The Environmentalist* 17, no. 1 (1997): 33–44; Roddy Scheer and Doug Moss, "Use It and Lose It: The Outsize Effect of U.S.

Consumption on the Environment," *Scientific American*, September 14, 2012, https://www.scientificamerican.com/article/american-consumption-habits/.

[26] Margot Adler, "Behind the Ever-Expanding American Dream House," NPR.org, July 4, 2006, https://www.npr.org/templates/story/story.php?storyId=5525283.

[27] Jon Mooallem, "The Self-Storage Self," *The New York Times*, September 2, 2009, sec. Magazine, https://www.nytimes.com/2009/09/06/magazine/06self-storage-t.html.

[28] Colton Gardner, "Self Storage Industry Statistics (2020)," *Neighbor Blog* (blog), December 18, 2019, https://www.neighbor.com/storage-blog/self-storage-industry-statistics/.

[29] Emma Johnson, "The Real Cost of Your Shopping Habits," *Forbes*, January 15, 2015, https://www.forbes.com/sites/emmajohnson/2015/01/15/the-real-cost-of-your-shopping-habits/.

[30] Mattias Wallander, "Closet Cast-Offs Clogging Landfills," *The Huffington Post*, May 25, 2011, https://www.huffpost.com/entry/closet-cast-offs-clogging_b_554400.

[31] Women Spend Eight Years of Their Life Shopping," *Dailymail.com*, November 27, 2006, https://www.dailymail.co.uk/fe-mail/article-419077/Women-spend-years-life-shopping.html.

[32] Megan Leonhardt, "55% of Americans with Credit Cards Have Debt—Here's How Much It Could Cost You," CNBC, May 20, 2019, https://www.cnbc.com/2019/05/17/55-percent-of-americans-have-credit-card-debt.html.

[33] Kaitlin Augustine, "Americans Aren't Minimalists, But Some Aspire to Be," *CivicScience*, August 27, 2018, https://civicscience.com/americans-arent-minimalists/.

[34] Lauren Davidson, "British Workers Are Skipping Lunch and That's Hurting Productivity," *The Telegraph*, January 6, 2015, https://www.telegraph.co.uk/finance/jobs/11326076/British-workers-are-skipping-lunch-and-thats-hurting-productivity.html.

[35] Jonathan Strum, "The Big Benzo: Unpacking Xanax Use in America," The Recovery Village Drug and Alcohol Rehab, October 5, 2020, https://www.therecoveryvillage.com/drug-addiction/news/use-in-america/.

[36] Benoit Denizet-Lewis, "Why Are More American Teenagers Than Ever Suffering From Severe Anxiety?," *The New York Times*, October 11, 2017, sec. Magazine, https://www.nytimes.com/2017/10/11/magazine/why-are-more-american-teenagers-than-ever-suffering-from-severe-anxiety.html.

[37] David Levine, "Are Some Age Groups More Prone to Depression Than Others?," *US News & World Report*, May 2, 2017, https://health.usnews.com/health-care/patient-advice/articles/2017-05-02/are-some-age-groups-more-prone-to-depression-than-others.

[38] "Alprazolam: Drug Usage Statistics, United States, 2008 - 2018," *ClinCalc.com*, January 18, 2021, https://clincalc.com/DrugStats/Drugs/Alprazolam.

[39] United States Congress Joint Economic Committee, "Long-Term Trends in Deaths of Despair," Social Capital Project (Washington, D.C., November 5, 2019), https://www.jec.senate.gov/public/_cache/files/0f2d3dba-9fdc-41e5-9bd1-9c13f4204e35/jec-report-deaths-of-despair.pdf.

[40] David Leonhardt and Stuart A. Thompson, "How Working-Class Life Is Killing Americans, in Charts," *The New York Times*, March 6, 2020, sec. Opinion, https://www.nytimes.com/interactive/2020/03/06/opinion/working-class-death-rate.html.

[41] United States Congress Joint Economic Committee, "Long-Term Trends in Deaths of Despair."

[42] Elizabeth Dwoskin, "Americans Might Never Go Back to the Office, and Twitter Is Leading the Charge," *The Washington Post*, October 1, 2020, sec. Technology, https://www.washingtonpost.com/technology/2020/10/01/twitter-work-from-home/; Shirin Ghaffary, "Facebook Is the Latest Major Tech Company to Let People Work

from Home Forever," *Vox*, May 21, 2020, https://www.vox.com/recode/2020/5/21/21266570/facebook-remote-work-from-home-mark-zuckerberg-twitter-covid-19-coronavirus.

[43] Alexander W. Bartik et al., "What Jobs Are Being Done at Home During the COVID-19 Crisis? Evidence from Firm-Level Surveys," Harvard Business School Entrepreneurial Management Working Papers 20, no. 138 (July 29, 2020): 27.

[44] Zameena Mejia, "Harvard's Longest Study of Adult Life Reveals How You Can Be Happier and More Successful," CNBC, March 20, 2018, https://www.cnbc.com/2018/03/20/this-harvard-study-reveals-how-you-can-be-happier-and-more-successful.html.

[45] "The Running List of 2020 Retail Bankruptcies," *Retail Dive*, February 5, 2021, https://www.retaildive.com/news/the-running-list-of-2020-retail-bankruptcies/571159/.

[46] Maggie Fitzgerald, "U.S. Savings Rate Hits Record 33% as Coronavirus Causes Americans to Stockpile Cash, Curb Spending," CNBC, May 29, 2020, https://www.cnbc.com/2020/05/29/us-savings-rate-hits-record-33percent-as-coronavirus-causes-americans-to-stockpile-cash-curb-spending.html.

[47] Karen Gilchrist, "These Millennials Are Reinventing the Multibillion-Dollar Education Industry during Coronavirus," CNBC, June 8, 2020, https://www.cnbc.com/2020/06/08/edtech-how-schools-education-industry-is-changing-under-coronavirus.html.

[48] Augustine, "Americans Aren't Minimalists."

[49] "How Many Ads Do You See Each Day?," GradSchools.com, September 12, 2018, https://www.gradschools.com/degree-guide/how-many-ads-do-you-see-each-day.

[50] Jennifer Kavanagh and Michael D. Rich, *Truth Decay: An Initial Exploration of the Diminishing Role of Facts and Analysis in American Public Life* (Rand Corporation, 2018).

[51] C. G. Jung, *Collected Works of C. G. Jung*, ed. Gerhard Adler and R. F. C. Hull, 2nd ed., vol. 9 (Part 1): "Archetypes and the Collective

Unconscious" (Princeton: Princeton University Press, 2014), 42.

[52] "Why Myth Matters," *Intercollegiate Studies Institute ISI Archive* (blog), April 21, 2014, https://isi.org/intercollegiate-review/why-myth-matters/.

[53] Christopher Vogler, *The Writer's Journey: Mythic Structure for Writers*, 3rd ed. (Studio City, CA: Michael Wiese Productions, 2007).

[54] John Zmirak, "The Generosity of Tolkien," *Crisis Magazine*, January 27, 2010, http://www.crisismagazine.com/2010/the-generosity-of-tolkien.

[55] Neil Gaiman, *The Books of Magic*, 30th Anniversary Edition (Burbank, CA: DC Comics, 2019).

[56] Adrienne LaFrance, "The Prophecies of Q," *The Atlantic*, June 2020, https://www.theatlantic.com/magazine/archive/2020/06/qanon-nothing-can-stop-what-is-coming/610567/.

[57] Fredric Jameson, *The Geopolitical Aesthetic: Cinema and Space in the World System* (Bloomington: Indiana University Press, 1992).

[58] Benjamin Frisch and Willa Paskin, "Decoder Ring: The Incunabula Papers: What Lies at the Heart of Ong's Hat?," *Slate,* October 29, 2018, https://slate.com/culture/2018/10/decoder-ring-explores-the-inter-dimensional-conspiracy-theory-known-as-ongs-hat-the-man-who-created-it-and-the-new-form-of-art-it-birthed.html.

[59] Eleanor Heartney, "Spirituality Has Long Been Erased From Art History. Here's Why It's Having a Resurgence Today," *Artnet News*, January 6, 2020, https://news.artnet.com/art-world/spirituality-and-art-resurgence-1737117.

[60] Guy Kawasaki, *Enchantment: The Art of Changing Hearts, Minds, and Actions* (New York: Penguin, 2011), 2.

[61] "Bruno Bettelheim: American Psychologist," in Encyclopedia Britannica, March 10, 2021, https://www.britannica.com/biography/Bruno-Bettelheim.

[62] Kawasaki, *Enchantment*, Chapter 1.

[63] Judith Rehak, "Tylenol Made a Hero of Johnson & Johnson: The Recall

That Started Them All," *The New York Times*, March 23, 2002, sec. Your Money, https://www.nytimes.com/2002/03/23/your-money/IHT-ty-lenol-made-a-hero-of-johnson-johnson-the-recall-that-started.html.

[64] "Spirituality," *Psychology Today,* accessed March 22, 2021, https://www.psychologytoday.com/us/basics/spirituality.

[65] Max Weber, *The Rational and Social Foundations of Music*, trans. Don Martindale, Johannes Riedel, and Gertrude Neuwirth (Carbondale: Southern Illinois University Press, 1958), xxi; note that the exact phrase "disenchantment of the world" originated from Friedrich Schiller.

[66] Rudolf Otto, *Autobiographical and Social Essays,* ed. Gregory D. Alles (Berlin: Walter de Gruyter, 1996), 30.

[67] William James, *The Varieties of Religious Experience: A Study in Human Nature,* Centenary Edition (London; New York: Routledge, 2002), 152; note that this exact quote originates from Maud Casey, The Art of Mystery: The Search for Questions (Graywolf Press, 2018), Chapter 1.

[68] Ann M. Pendleton-Jullian, Mapping the Pragmatic Imagination: An Interview with Ann M. Pendleton-Jullian (Part Two), interview by Henry Jenkins, November 21, 2016, http://henryjenkins.org/blog/2016/11/mapping-the-pragmatic-imagination-an-interview-with-ann-m-pendleton-jullian-part-two.html.

[69] "Samsung Electronics Becomes Top Five in Interbrand's Best Global brands 2020," October 20, 2020, https://news.samsung.com/global/samsung-electronics-becomes-top-five-in-interbrands-best-global-brands-2020.

[70] "Brands and Brand Names," Inc.com, May 1, 2021, https://www.inc.com/encyclopedia/brands-and-brand-names.html.

[71] Ivan Stevanovic, "How Many ECommerce Sites Are There in 2020?," *KommandoTech* (blog), February 13, 2020, https://kommandotech.com/statistics/how-many-ecommerce-sites-are-there/.

[72] Erin Duffin, "Total Number of Patents Issued in the U.S. FY 2000-FY 2020," *Statista,* November 19, 2020, https://www.statista.com/

statistics/256571/number-of-patent-grants-in-the-us/.

[73] Carr, "How Many Ads Do We See A Day?"

[74] "GEICO's Advertising Spending Slows But Still Tops $1 Billion: SNL," *Insurance Journal*, March 20, 2014, https://www.insurancejournal.com/news/national/2014/03/20/323788.htm.

[75] Simon & Garfunkel, Bridge Over Troubled Water (New York: Columbia Records, 1970).

[76] Edward S. Rogers, "Some Historical Matter Concerning Trade-Marks," *Michigan Law Review* 9, no. 1 (1910): 29–43, https://doi.org/10.2307/1276308.

[77] Quoted in Bruce Orwall, Brian Steinberg, and Joann S. Lublin, "Eisner Steps Down as Disney Chairman," *The Wall Street Journal*, March 4, 2004, sec. News, https://www.wsj.com/articles/SB107832734296045356.

[78] Joseph S. Nye, Jr., *Soft Power: The Means To Success In World Politics* (New York: PublicAffairs, 2005), 2.

[79] Maja Pawinska Sims, "CEOs Play A Crucial Role In Enhancing & Maintaining brand Value, Global Study Finds," PRovoke, January 24, 2019, https://www.provokemedia.com/latest/article/ceos-play-a-crucial-role-in-enhancing-maintaining-brand-value-global-study-finds.

[80] https://www.visualcapitalist.com/the-most-loved-brands/

[81] For more details, see Akhilesh Ganti, "Economic Moat," Investopedia, March 21, 2020, https://www.investopedia.com/terms/e/economicmoat.asp.

[82] Drake Baer, "How Only Being Able to Use Logic to Make Decisions Destroyed a Man's Life," *The Cut*, June 14, 2016, https://www.thecut.com/2016/06/how-only-using-logic-destroyed-a-man.html; see also Antonio R. Damasio, *Descartes' Error: Emotion, Reason, and the Human Brain* (New York: Penguin, 1994).

[83] Lt. J.g. Doug Masters, "Night Carrier Qualifications," *Flying*, July 12, 2007, http://www.flyingmag.com/pilot-reports/jets/night-carrier-qualifications/.

[84] Carolyn Dewar, Martin Hirt, and Scott Keller, "The Mindsets and Practices of Excellent CEOs," MicKinsey & Company, October 25, 2019, http://ceros.mckinsey.com/the-next-normal-callout.

[85] Audrey Choi, "How Younger Investors Could Reshape the World," Morgan Stanley, January 24, 2018, https://www.morganstanley.com/access/why-millennial-investors-are-different.

[86] Nadia Cameron, "How National Geographic Is Innovating Its Brand with Purpose," *CMO Australia*, March 23, 2017, https://www.cmo.com.au/article/616491/how-national-geographic-building-brand-purpose-led-future/.

87 "Johnson & Johnson," Vault.com, accessed March 23, 2021, https://www.vault.com/company-profiles/personal-care/johnson-johnson.

[88] Lewis Carroll, A*lice's Adventures in Wonderland and Through the Looking Glass* (Reader's Library Classics, 2021), 180.

[89] Octavio Paz, *The Siren and the Seashell: And Other Essays on Poets and Poetry*, trans. Lysander Kemp and Margaret Sayers Peden (Austin: University of Texas Press, 2013), Part III.

[90] Alex McDowell, "Alex McDowell, R.D.I.," USC School of Cinematic Arts | World Building Media Lab, accessed March 23, 2021, https://worldbuilding.usc.edu/people/bio/alex-mcdowell/.

[91] Alex McDowell, "About," USC School of Cinematic Arts | World Building Media Lab, accessed March 23, 2021, https://worldbuilding.institute/about.

[92] Pendleton-Jullian and Brown, *Design Unbound*, 1:148–149.

[93] Howard Schultz, *Pour Your Heart into It: How Starbucks Built a Company One Cup at a Time* (New York: Hachette Books, 2012), Chapter 18.

[94] "Culture of Purpose," Deloitte, accessed March 23, 2021, https://www2.deloitte.com/us/en/pages/about-deloitte/articles/culture-of-purpose.html.

[95] Quoted in Sims, "CEOs Play A Crucial Role in Enhancing & Maintaining brand Value."

[96] Guy Kawasaki, "Are You a CEO ... 'Chief Enchantment Officer'??," Vistage Research Center, January 26, 2012, https://www.vistage.com/research-center/personal-development/leadership-competencies/are-you-a-ceo-chief-enchantment-officer/.

[97] Quoted in Sims, "CEOs Play A Crucial Role In Enhancing & Maintaining Brand Value."

[98] Quoted in Sims.

[99] Punit Renjen, "What Really Drives Employee Engagement?," ChiefExecutive.net, January 24, 2013, https://chiefexecutive.net/what-really-drives-employee-engagement/.

[100] Susan Sorenson and Keri Garman, "How to Tackle U.S. Employees' Stagnating Engagement," Gallup.com, June 11, 2013, https://news.gallup.com/businessjournal/162953/tackle-employees-stagnating-engagement.aspx.

[101] Renjen, "What Really Drives Employee Engagement?"

[102] John R. Graham et al., "Corporate Culture: Evidence from the Field" (National Bureau of Economic Research, March 20, 2017), https://www.nber.org/papers/w23255.

[103] Natalie Baumgartner, "Build a Culture That Aligns with People's Values," *Harvard Business Review*, April 8, 2020, https://hbr.org/2020/04/build-a-culture-that-aligns-with-peoples-values.

[104] Kawasaki, "Chief Enchantment Officer."

[105] T. J. McCue, "57 Million U.S. Workers Are Part of the Gig Economy," *Forbes*, August 31, 2018, https://www.forbes.com/sites/tjmccue/2018/08/31/57-million-u-s-workers-are-part-of-the-gig-economy/.

[106] Aaron Smith, "Gig Work, Online Selling and Home Sharing," Pew Research Center: Internet & Technology, November 17, 2016, https://www.pewresearch.org/internet/2016/11/17/gig-work-online-selling-and-home-sharing/; see also Abha Bhattarai, "Now Hiring, for a One-Day Job: The Gig Economy Hits Retail," *Washington Post*, May 4, 2018, sec. Business, https://www.washingtonpost.com/

business/economy/now-hiring-for-a-one-day-job-the-gig-economy-hits-retail/2018/05/04/2bebdd3c-4257-11e8-ad8f-27a8c409298b_story.html.

[107] Andrew S. Gillis, "What Is the Gig Economy?," WhatIs.com, accessed March 24, 2021, https://whatis.techtarget.com/definition/gig-economy.

[108] Ivy Wigmore, "What Is Flexible Workforce?," WhatIs.com, September 1, 2016, https://whatis.techtarget.com/definition/flexible-workforce.

[109] Diane Mulcahy, "Who Wins in the Gig Economy, and Who Loses," *Harvard Business Review*, October 27, 2016, https://hbr.org/2016/10/who-wins-in-the-gig-economy-and-who-loses.

[110] Douglas Holtz-Eakin, Ben Gitis, and Will Rinehart, "The Gig Economy: Research and Policy Implications of Regional, Economic, and Demographic Trends," Future of Work Initiative & American Action Forum (The Aspen Institute, January 2017), 4, https://www.aspeninstitute.org/wp-content/uploads/2017/02/Regional-and-Industry-Gig-Trends-2017.pdf.

[111] Staffing Industry Analysts, "Total Spending on US Gig Work Close to $800 Billion," *PR Newswire*, September 21, 2016, https://www.prnewswire.com/news-releases/total-spending-on-us-gig-work-close-to-800-billion-300331650.html.

[112] Holtz-Eakin, Gitis, and Rinehart, "The Gig Economy," 14–16.

[113] "Tips for Building Your Personal brand," *Northeastern University Graduate Programs* (blog), January 14, 2019, https://www.northeastern.edu/graduate/blog/tips-for-building-your-personal-brand/.

[114] Meero Team, "11 Dos & Donts for Your LinkedIn Profile Picture in 2020," Meero.com, July 16, 2020, https://www.meero.com/en/news/corporate/411/11-Tips-To-Follow-For-The-Perfect-Linkedin-Profile-Picture-In-2019.

[115] Matt Singer, "Welcome to the 2015 Recruiter Nation, Formerly Known as the Social Recruiting Survey," *Jobvite*, September 22, 2015, https://www.jobvite.com/blog/jobvite-news-and-reports/

welcome-to-the-2015-recruiter-nation-formerly-known-as-the-so-cial-recruiting-survey/.

[116] "Tips for Building Your Personal brand."

[117] Pendleton-Jullian and Brown, Design Unbound, 2:252.

[118] Marsha Kinder, *Playing With Power in Movies, Television, and Video Games: From Muppet Babies to Teenage Mutant Ninja Turtles* (University of California Press, 1991), Chapter 2.

[119] Peter Weir, *Dead Poets Society* (Buena Vista Pictures Distribution, 1989).

[120] Martin A. Nowak, "Five Rules for the Evolution of Cooperation," *Science* 314, no. 5805 (December 8, 2006): 1560–63.

[121] A. J. Willis, "The Ecosystem: An Evolving Concept Viewed Historically," *Functional Ecology* 11, no. 2 (1997): 268–71.

[122] James F. Moore, "Predators and Prey: A New Ecology of Competition," *Harvard Business Review,* June 1993, https://hbr.org/1993/05/predators-and-prey-a-new-ecology-of-competition.

[123] James F. Moore, *The Death of Competition: Leadership and Strategy in the Age of Business Ecosystems* (New York: HarperBusiness, 1996), 26.

[124] Jack Fuller, Michael G. Jacobides, and Martin Reeves, "The Myths and Realities of Business Ecosystems," *MIT Sloan Management Review,* February 25, 2019, https://sloanreview.mit.edu/article/the-myths-and-realities-of-business-ecosystems/.

[125] https://penzu.com/

[126] Pendleton-Jullian and Brown, Design Unbound, 1:ix–x.

[127] Pendleton-Jullian and Brown, 2:414.

[128] Émile Durkheim, *The Elementary Forms of Religious Life, trans. Carol Cosman* (Oxford: Oxford University Press, 2008), 280.

[129] Maurice Halbwachs, *On Collective Memory,* trans. Lewis A. Coser (Chicago: University of Chicago Press, 1992), 82.

[130] George Sylvester Viereck, "What Life Means to Einstein," *The Saturday Evening Post,* October 26, 1929, 117, http://www.saturdayeveningpost.com/wp-content/uploads/satevepost/what_life_means_to_einstein.pdf.

Index

A

Accenture, 163, 237
Acura, 68, 237
Airbnb, 101, 201, 237
Alexa, xii, 211, 237
American Airlines, 237, 244
American Express, 53, 66, 80, 83, 128–129, 235, 237
American Idol, 106, 237
AOL, 237
Apple, 53, 57–58, 67, 72, 80, 83, 91, 96, 104, 106, 111–112, 129–130, 160–161, 178, 202, 217, 237, 242
AT&T, 69, 111, 116, 132, 235, 237
Avis, 69, 111, 237
Avon, 89, 237

B

Batman, 43, 237
Bayer, 156, 237
Behance, 176, 237
Birds Eye Foods, 62, 237
Bitcoin, 100, 237
Black Rifle Coffee, 58, 132, 237
BMW, 68–69, 83, 85, 202, 237
Brooks Brothers, 26, 237
Budweiser, 155, 237
Burger King, 83, 155, 238, 243

C

Campbell's Soup, 66
Chanel, 126, 217, 238
Club Med, 193, 238
Coca-Cola, 83, 132, 238
Corona, 132, 238
Coursera, 29, 238
Culture Vulture, 147, 238

D

Dell, 89, 238
Deloitte, 83, 165–167, 223, 238, 255
Delta, 70, 238
Disney, 43, 53, 58, 79, 82–83, 164, 229, 238, 254
Dixie Cups, 62, 238
DÔEN, 129–130, 238
Dove, 85, 238
Dungeons and Dragons, 152, 238
Dunkin' Donuts, 178, 238

E

E-ZPass, 238
Equinox, 201, 238
Esso, 62, 235, 238
Estée Lauder, 62, 238
Exxon, 49, 83, 115–116, 235, 238

F

Federal Express, 82, 238
Fender, 202, 239
Fiji Water, 239
Firestone, 62, 239
Four Seasons, 164, 201, 239
Frodo Baggins, 43, 239
Fujifilm, 82, 239

G

Gap, 33, 42, 46, 165–166, 169, 239
Gatorade, 85, 137, 239
Geico, 72, 226, 239, 254
Glass, 83, 222, 239, 255
Godfather's Pizza, 151, 239
Google, 1, 83, 100, 179, 186, 239
Goop, 202, 239
Grey Goose, 163, 239

H

Hallmark, 111, 239
Harley Davidson, 58, 69, 239
Harry Potter, 152, 239
Heineken, 82, 239
Hertz, 69, 82, 239
Hewlett-Packard, 89, 239
Honda, 68, 237, 239
Huggies, 90–91, 240

I

IBM, 89, 106, 235, 240
Igloo, 66, 240

Instagram, 15, 184, 240
Intel, 53, 82, 160, 240
Ivory Soap, 82, 240

J

J. Crew, 240
J.C. Penney, 26, 240
Jeep, 62, 68, 74, 132, 202, 240
JetBlue, 70, 112, 240
John Deere, 111, 125–126, 240
Johnson & Johnson, 57, 80, 91, 96, 106, 128, 156, 160, 230, 232, 240, 252, 255

K

Kellogg, 62, 240, 243
Kmart, 85, 240
Kodak, 12, 82, 240

L

L.S./M.F.T., 240
Land, 106, 127, 240
Lego, 82, 240
LENS, 2, 12, 67–68, 71, 76–77, 106, 175, 240
LG, 240
LinkedIn, 182–184, 228, 240, 257
LMI, 193, 240
Lord & Taylor, 26, 240
Lord of the Rings, 43, 152, 240
Lucky brand, 26, 240
Lucky Strike, 62, 241

Luke Skywalker, 43, 241
LuluLemon, 201, 241

M

Marlboro, 70, 82, 125, 137, 241
Mastercard, 129, 241
McDonalds, 241
MCI, 58, 241
McKinsey, 122, 223, 241, 255
Mercedes Benz, 68, 241
Merck, 106, 156, 241
Michelin, 85, 241
Microsoft, 80, 91, 241
Miller, 85, 241
Minority Report, 152–153, 241
MTV, 89, 241

N

Narnia, 152, 241
National Geographic, 127, 222, 241, 255
NAVAIR, 131, 151, 241
Neiman Marcus, 26, 241
NetJets, 201, 241
Newton, 83, 242
Nike, 53, 67, 83, 91, 104, 108, 116, 130–131, 137, 173, 178, 217, 242

O

OpenTable, 242
Oprah, 202, 242
Orvis, 129, 202, 242

P

Pampers, 90–91, 242
Pan Am, 68, 242
Patagonia, 83, 107, 126–127, 242
Pella, 111, 242
Pepsi, 66, 83, 242
Pier 1 Imports, 242
Play-Doh, 66, 242
Poland Spring, 242
Porsche, 74, 242
Prius, 74, 242
Prodigy, 68, 242

Q

Qwest, 58, 111, 127–128, 235, 242

R

Ralph Lauren, 132, 242
RAND, 39, 145, 180, 201, 226, 236, 242, 251
RC Cola, 83, 242
REI, 164, 242
Rocky Mountain Sparkling Water, 83, 242

S

Samsung, 70–71, 230, 235, 243, 253
Satisfries, 83, 243
Shinola, 111, 243
Skillshare, 29, 243
Smile Direct Club, 106, 243

Snap Crackle Pop, 62, 243

Snickers, 85, 137, 243

Sony, 70–71, 243

Southwest Airlines, 106, 243

Spanx, 160, 243

Sparks & Honey, 147, 243

Spider-Man, 43, 243

Sprint, 58, 243

Star Trek, 90, 243

Star Wars, 43, 152, 243

Starbucks, 83, 107, 112, 151, 172, 230, 243, 255

Stay Curious, 193, 243

Sur la Table, 26, 243

Surf, 68, 243

Suzuki, 243

T

Tesla, 33, 243

The Dead Poets Society, 194

The Matrix, 152, 243

The New York Times, 19, 131–132, 223, 227–228, 230, 243, 249–250, 253

The Paper Store, 26, 244

Tide, 68, 86, 244

Tiffany, 58, 65, 82, 244

Toptal, 176, 244

Trend Hunter, 147, 244

TripAdvisor, 201, 244

True Religion, 26, 244

Twitter, 25, 182, 184, 223, 244, 250–251

Tylenol, 57, 83, 96, 106, 230, 244, 252–253

U

U.S. Airways, 244

Uber, 100, 244

United Airlines, 244

V

Venmo, 66, 201, 244

Virgin, 160, 164, 244

Virgin Air, 244

Visa, 66, 244

Volvo, 68, 85, 244

W

Walmart, 65, 85, 97, 244

Weight Watchers, 136, 244

Whole Foods, 201–202, 244

World of Warcraft, 152, 244

WW, 136, 244

X

Xanax, 19, 231, 245, 250

Y

Yamaha, 245

Yeti, 58, 66, 245

Z

Zoom, 25, 245

Made in the USA
Las Vegas, NV
22 February 2022

44388091R00163